pots & plants

MITCHELL BEAZLEY

pots & plants

INSPIRED YEAR-ROUND IDEAS FOR YOUR OUTSIDE SPACE

Barbara Segall

WITH PHOTOGRAPHY BY CLIVE NICHOLS

pots & plants
Barbara Segall

First published in Great Britain in 2006
by Mitchell Beazley, an imprint of
Octopus Publishing Group Ltd
2–4 Heron Quays, London E14 4JP
An Hachette Livre UK Company
www.octopusbooks.co.uk

First published in paperback in 2008

A CIP catalogue copy of this book is available from the
British Library

ISBN: 978 1 84533 361 4

Commissioning Editor: Michèle Byam
Art Editor: Victoria Burley
Senior Editor: Peter Taylor
Copy Editor: Naomi Waters
Design: Nigel Soper
Production: Jane Rogers
Proofreader: Clare Peel
Index: Sue Farr

Printed and bound in China by
Toppan Printing Company Limited

introduction

WHETHER YOUR GARDEN IS MEASURED IN ACRES OR FEET, PLANTED POTS WILL BE ONE OF ITS FEATURES. YOU DON'T HAVE TO BE A LARGE-SCALE GARDENER WITH A HUGE GARDEN TO ENJOY GROWING FLOWERS, HERBS, FRUITS AND VEGETABLES, TREES AND SHRUBS... AND YOU CAN GROW THEM ALL IN THE SMALL SPACE OF POTS.

As you are providing for all the basic needs of your potted collection you have a more or less unlimited choice of plants. Your choice of plants isn't as restricted – as it might be in beds and borders – by the type of soil, the aspect of your garden and its microclimate. And, if you have no garden soil at all, as in a basement area or roof garden, you can pick and choose, creating a potted garden to suit the site.

Even if you have a large garden and space is not a constraint, container gardens can be used as part of the whole, while in a smaller garden, containers often comprise the whole of the garden.

Pots offer a flexible and adaptable growing area. Provided they are not too heavy to move easily, you can shift pots from place to place to vary the look of a particular planting. With a container garden, you can chop and change the outdoor scene from season to season, or you can create displays that have elements of each season and change as the year progresses. The moveability of pots means that you can bring any tender plants out into the open for the summer, and return them to frost-free conditions for the winter.

Pots are available in many different materials that suit different garden styles. You can choose terracotta, lead, or wood for more traditional displays, and metal, plastic, and stone for a more contemporary look. You can also customize and decorate terracotta, wood, and plastic pots to suit your own individual style.

On special occasions, you can add to your existing displays or create new ones, using spur-of-the-moment purchases of seasonal plants from garden centres or nurseries, to create stylish planted pots just for a particular event.

Setting the scene

I like to think of plants in pots as actors on a stage. Perennial plants and evergreen, foliage shrubs and trees that survive in all weathers are there for the longest run of all. Others, the short-term, seasonal plants such as bulbs and annuals, offer an effervescent quality to the display. They fizz and sparkle but are only here for the cheers at curtain call during their short-run performance.

I see the container gardener as the stage manager, waiting in the wings to prompt and prop-up those that forget their lines or get in a muddle... and naturally you have to pamper them and treat them as the stars that they are. But you also have to remember that when one seasonal scene has been played out, you need to make sure that there are plenty of other new cast members waiting in the wings, ready for encores and curtain calls.

OPPOSITE
This dramatic row of tall, colourful pots is an architectural feature in its own right – incidentally relieving the utility of the garage wall – and the pots are tall and bright enough to be clearly visible to drivers! For tall pots choose squat plants that have plenty of growth at the base, such as *Carex muskingumensis*, the daisy-like *Erigeron* 'Nachthimmel' and *Phormium* 'Platt's Black', all of which offer variations of colour and texture.

Treat each season as an act in a year-round theatrical extravaganza of colour, texture, and even perfume. In order to maintain the continuity of the spectacle, you may need to have extras and understudies waiting in the wings, ready to come on show when each season's stars begin to show the stresses and strains of their round-the-clock performances.

The drama of the container garden relies on plants and pots, and how these two elements are combined to achieve the most stunning effects. To get this right you need to choose from the myriad of different pots that come in all shapes, sizes, and materials.

Pots filled to overflowing with plants will provide strong visual interest. The plants you choose will provide the necessary changes in height as they grow to fill the space, but you can add interest to the collection by arranging the pots on tiered metal *étagères*. The sky is literally the limit with pot plants, as you can fix pots to walls, iron stairways, balconies, and window-ledges.

And then there are the plants themselves. Container gardeners should never feel deprived of plant opportunities; rather, you will be spoilt for choice.

Star plants

There are so many different types of plants you could choose to use. Think of every situation in the garden and the plants you would choose for those sites; then think "pots", and you will find that you can create a "garden-in-pot" to suit your garden's needs, or to decorate patios, balconies, and basement yards.

There are permanent plantings of architectural plants such as phormiums and bay trees. There are the shady characters that can enliven dark, cool areas; the sunbathers, which thrive in hotspots; the high flyers, which sprint up any support you offer them and provide you with colour and texture at different heights. Then there are the annuals, such as petunias and pansies, which explode with colour in spring and summer, like star-burst fireworks: they are like floral fountains that cascade over the rims of pots. As do the trailers, which soften the edges of their containers, providing a complete wrap-around quality to some plantings. In addition, there are the stand-alone, specimen plants, with strong architectural qualities, which look best unaccompanied by other plants. And then there are the "fuss pots", which need special soils or feeding regimes.

You can grow climbers, including sweet peas and clematis, against walls, fences, or trellis, or even, if you choose lower-growing varieties, to suit a tabletop on a patio. There are trees and shrubs, and herbaceous perennials that offer flowers, foliage, and berries or attractive bark at different times during the growing season. You can also grow vegetables, fruit, and herbs in containers, so, even if you only have a small outdoor space, you can still grow your own fruit and vegetables, which will no doubt taste sweeter and fresher than their shop-bought equivalents.

OPPOSITE
Use pots to mark the edge of garden steps – they can hide what is often an awkward spot and visually help to soften the hard surfaces. Choose plants such as the ornamental grass (*Pennisetum alopecuroides*) that arch downwards to draw the attention to the garden below. It's a good idea to have another set of plants in pots, growing on, waiting in the wings to replace the first set once they have passed their best.

You can see your contained garden as permanent or temporary; ring the changes as and when you want, bringing in new colour schemes and creating new moods, from season to season, or even from day to day. Large pots and plants are, by virtue of their size, more permanent. Anything else you can treat as ephemeral – here today for a particular occasion and moved on tomorrow or the next day, when you want a quick change of scene on the patio. Because you can buy plants in containers all year round, you can almost treat container gardening as a more robust form of flower arranging; you can group together plants that might not live happily together for the long term, but will co-exist for the duration of a special occasion.

Potted plants are ideal for creating instant colour in areas of the garden or courtyard where you cannot grow plants successfully in the ground. You can also use pots as you would a statue or sundial, as highlights and focal points. They can be used to mark the boundaries of particular areas of the garden, or to lead your eye into another area, but, more importantly, wherever you use them, they will fill the space with colour and texture.

Pots are useful for bringing seasonal highlights or colourful flowers into areas of the garden where they would otherwise not be able to grow, such as in places where existing shrubs are too densely planted to allow any new plants to compete successfully, or where it is possibly too dark to grow them in the ground. They can be brought in to spaces such as these for the short term.

Create a style

You can create the look that suits the overall surroundings and structure of your garden; alternatively, you can use a potted collection to create a contrasting feature in a small area of the garden. Modern, traditional, informal and formal: by choosing plants and pots to complement each other, you can install a design that fits the particular moment or that is more permanent. In addition, you can choose a colour scheme, a style , and seasonal themes, all to suit your planting personality.

You can achieve different visual effects depending on the scale of display you create. A mass of pots, just one huge example, or a collection of several medium-sized pots – whatever scale of arrangement you choose, the results promise to be dramatic and eye-catching.

Work with the seasons, thinking ahead, so that you have the perfect plant and pot combinations to provide you with containers bursting with vibrant colour and subtle textures, from foliage, flowers, berries, and stems. To set you on your way, there are several projects that follow the seasonal chapters in this book. They show how the plants that enliven spring, early and late summer, autumn and winter can be used to create stylish and thematic container collections that will transform your displays throughout the year.

OPPOSITE
Graceful, yet spiky, *Cordyline australis* plays a leading role in this dramatic scene. In summer, double-flowered, deep orange nasturtium tumbles through its sword-like leaves, over the rim of the container and trails down the brick pedestal. The whole planting offers a strong focal point at the end of a low brick wall.

choosing pots and plants

pot sizes, shapes, styles, and materials

CHOOSE POTS FOR THEIR SIZE, SHAPE, TEXTURE AND COLOUR, TO AMASS A COLLECTION THAT SUITS THE CHARACTER OF YOUR GARDEN SPACE AND ADDS ZING TO YOUR INDIVIDUAL GARDEN STYLE.

Plants will grow in just about any sort of container, provided that it has drainage holes, and you supply the compost and drainage materials. The choice is there for the making, and the range of pots available is vast. Garden centres pile them high, and there is a shape, size, texture, style, and colour that is sure to suit the site, the plants, and you.

If you want a modern style, there are contemporary and funky pots that will offer the look you are seeking. If the house and garden have a traditional feel, then choose one of the traditional and timeless favourite types of containers. And, of course, if the pot you choose is plain, you can paint or decorate it to co-ordinate with the house or patio walls, or vice versa – you could paint the walls to match or pick out the colour of the pots you use.

You can make a large and showy display with a collection of small pots; a strong and bold architectural statement with a single, big, stylish pot, while a shapely, but empty, one offers ornamental possibilities beyond its primary use as a container for plants. Small, medium, large,

ultra-large, and architectural sizes are all available. There are pots in so many different sizes, not to mention materials, that you have ample opportunity to add distinctive style to your outdoor space.

The size of the pots that you use is dictated by the space you have available, and by the type of plant, or combination of plants, you want to put into each container. In a limited space, you should have one large and abundant planting in one generous-sized container. Alternatively, you might choose to combine several different pots of varying sizes to achieve a "border" effect. You need to have a sense of proportion. Small pots make a small space look even

PREVIOUS PAGE
Choose your pots and plants to reflect your personal style. Here, unadorned, geometric containers match the plain, rectangular shapes, flat surfaces, and repeating texture of the contemporary-style house and garden. Shade- and moisture-loving hostas nestle in the smaller cube pond pot, while stately arum lilies (*Zantedeschia aethiopica*) occupy the larger one. Lining the water feature are rendered-concrete troughs planted with bold and contrasting foliage of ferns and tiarellas, and colourful vegetables.

OPPOSITE
With or without plants, a cleverly placed, shapely terracotta pot adds a hint of antiquity to a relaxed border planting, blending well with the flower and foliage colours of valerian, rue, oleander, germander and iris.

smaller, while a large pot filled with a colourful mixture of bedding and evergreen permanent plants will counter-balance the small space in which it sits.

Weight and height

On a balcony or a roof-top garden, the weight of pots when filled with compost and plants will be a critical factor. Before you start to design a potted garden on a roof-top, it's wise to check out local planning regulations, ideally with a qualified structural surveyor or a building surveyor. Once you've received the go-ahead you can decide on what sort of pots to choose.

BELOW
Weight down the bases of tall metallic pots so that they won't topple over when the leafy arum lily plants are buffeted by wind on this roof-top. The plants are set in their own smaller containers, while the pebble mulch on the surface hides the pot rims.

ABOVE
Finely cut and arching, the straw-coloured foliage of *Carex comans* complements the metallic smoothness of this rounded bowl-like cache pot.

RIGHT
It's hard to tell if this is a faux-lead or a traditional lead planter. Either way, it is the perfect partner for a collection of traditional container plants – pelargoniums – which are available in a range of flower colours and leaf types to give the pot added interest.

Medium-sized, wide plastic or resin-mixture pots filled with lightweight, multi-purpose compost are ideal. The larger the pot, the more compost it will hold, and although this will be good for growing an interesting combination of plants, it will mean that once planted up, it will not lend itself to being moved from place to place should you decide to rearrange your garden. If you do choose large and heavy pots, you will need a sack trolley or castors to move the pots at a later date. When you site the pots make sure that they are placed on areas of the roof that are load-bearing.

Some large pots are available with false floors, which you can insert into the pot at varying heights so that you don't have to fill the whole, huge space with compost. If the container doesn't have its own false floor, you can improvise and recycle packaging materials such as polystyrene. Put something weighty, such as a layer of gravel, which will be good for drainage into the base of the pot, to anchor it down. Then fill the pot with polystyrene foam, either in bead form or broken into small chunks, up to the level at which you want the compost to start.

Although the gravel adds some degree of weight, the lightness of the polystyrene will offset it, and together they will provide good drainage and reduce the amount of compost needed for the large pots.

You can achieve the same effect with a home-made wire basket to support a smaller pot, which you can then place inside the larger pot. Mould a layer of chicken wire, so that it fits into the neck of the outer pot, with a small section hooked over the pot rim. This will support the smaller pot and make it simple to remove when its flowering or growing season is over, without disturbing any of the material that you have used for weighting, draining, and packing out the taller pot.

Tall, wide-shouldered pots are useful to give height and solidity to a group of containers. They also lend themselves to showing off trailing foliage plants such as ivy and the silver-leaved *Dichondra* 'Silver Fall's', as well as cascading flowering plants, such as petunias and nasturtiums. The foliage and flowers of these plants hang over the rims of tall pots, flowing down the sides in arching trails, softening the edges and increasing the ornamental quality of any pot collections. In addition, tall pots have a practical use: they suit plants such as lilies and clematis, as

OPPOSITE
An empty pot nestling in a bed of planted specimens serves to catch the eye and provide a textural contrast.

BELOW
Custom-made though it is, the uncomplicated shape of this pot, offers a satisfying symmetry. Instead of using it for plants, it has become part of the styling of the patio it colour-matches. Fill it daily with fresh water to provide an oasis for birds and to offer reflections of the surroundings into the garden. You could also use it as a temporary vase and float individual flowers and foliage, highlights of the moment, in the water.

these plants perform better if they have a cool, deep root run.

Materials

I prefer using terracotta pots, as this warm, mellow material always brings to mind the balmy warmth of the Mediterranean, and reminds me of patios and balconies that I have enjoyed in Portugal, Spain, Italy, and France. Terracotta is a lovely material to use as it "breathes", keeping the plant roots cool, and, because the clay is porous, there is no chance that they will become waterlogged. Its properties and its appearance suit many drought-tolerant plants, such as thyme, oleander, lavender, and *Osteospermum*.

Terracotta pots are heavy when filled with moist compost, so you need to think carefully about weight on roofs and balconies. Also make sure you buy terracotta pots that are guaranteed to be frost-resistant.

Plastic pots in black, green, or a ruddy, clay colour are widely available in varying sizes and of course are inexpensive. You will also find plastic pots with mouldings and markings that mimic terracotta so well that it is hard to spot the difference.

RIGHT
Steely-grey and arching, the foliage of *Astelia chathamica*, a tender perennial, is well and truly earthed by the smooth, warm terracotta of the container.

OPPOSITE
Suffering from artistic metal fatigue, this one-off "saggy pot", holding a reviving clump of French lavender (*Lavandula stoechas*) makes a humorous corner-piece. The grey foliage of the lavender combines well with the pot, and its flower colour tones with the colour of the patio walls.

ABOVE
Large plants, such as the Himalayan birch (*Betula utilis*), need large containers to hold sufficient compost to keep them growing well.

OPPOSITE TOP
A courtyard at Keukenhof Gardens in The Netherlands provides a sheltered spot for immense white pots of tulips, planted up according to variety. Beside the bench in the foreground, grape hyacinth are mixed with ornamental onion (*Allium karataviense*) and pale-lavender violas.

OPPOSITE BOTTOM
Beautiful as they can be when full, tall pots with narrow shoulders are often best left as stand-alone sculptural objects rather than used as plant containers, since repotting can be very difficult.

Fibreglass and resin pots are finished to look like weathered terracotta, stone, or lead. Pots made from these materials are frost-proof and relatively maintenance-free, although plastic can become brittle, and may then crack.

They are all lightweight and easy to handle, so even when filled they can be moved around from place to place with relative ease. The sides of these pots are not porous, so they need less frequent watering, but they can get too hot and bake the roots of the plants they hold.

Galvanized iron and other metallic containers are popular for modern-looking areas and for use in more avant-garde designs. They are attractive in their own right and enhance the ornamental look of the planting as a whole; however, they are not good insulators for the plants in cold weather and in hot weather they may act like heat conductors, baking the compost and the roots of plants. If they do not have drainage holes, you will either have to drill them in yourself, or decide to use the container as a cover pot or cache pot for an inner container.

Lead boxes and planters are among the most traditional of containers, but the real thing is very expensive. Fortunately, there are some faux-lead containers that look like the real thing, but, being made from lighter materials, they are more versatile and less expensive.

You may be lucky and find iron containers such as tanks or baths from architectural salvage firms.

The interiors will need to be treated to prevent them from rusting when in contact with moist compost.

Wooden boxes and barrels are popular choices for container plantings. Wood is natural, and, like terracotta, it breathes and offers insulation to plants from extremes of hot and cold. Wooden containers need to be treated with a paint finish or wood preservative before planting.

Barrels are usually treated with a charcoal burn, so that the interior won't rot. Many barrels are made from oak, so are long-lasting. They are large, and heavy when filled, so make sure you site them well before planting up.

Wooden boxes are often used as cache pots. The best examples are rectangular conservatory boxes, sometimes called Versailles or Paris boxes, and they look at their formal best holding pots that in turn hold lemon or orange trees, as well as other large specimen trees or shrubs. Their formal appreance suits traditional topiary.

Glazed pots are a delight to use, as they come in a huge range of colours and styles and combine well with plants and other elements of garden decoration. The glazed surface is easy to wipe clean, so keeps disease and some pests, such as slugs and snails, off the plants. You can choose which shape and colour fits with the style of planting you aim to create. Like terracotta pots, glazed ones need to be handled carefully, as they can chip. Once a glazed pot is damaged it is likely to be a liability in winter.

Unlike terracotta pots, glazed ones are not porous, so plants will need to be watered carefully, to avoid waterlogging. They may not be frost-proof, so check before buying, and make sure that there are drainage holes in the bases of the pots.

Reconstituted stone is a natural-looking material, with a good finish, making it suitable for formal plantings. It is relatively inexpensive, but is heavy. It is best to plant it up in situ and use it for semi-permanent plantings. It is frost-resistant, but may take a couple of seasons to age and look weathered.

Concrete pots are available in a wide range of shapes, all with varied exterior detailing, such as swags and handles, and many are made to mimic stone containers. Concrete is a strong material, so pots are not likely to crack or be damaged in handling. It is frost-resistant, but in winter it will be cool, so you may need to provide some insulation, especially for smaller containers. Size and weight make concrete containers suitable for semi-permanent plantings. They are heavy to move and so need to be planted up in their growing positions. The interior should be treated with a sealant before planting up, so check when you buy if this has already been done.

OPPOSITE
Tall pots, like these slim, textured, concrete containers, need to be securely positioned so they cannot be dislodged. Play with perspective by matching pots with different-sized plants.

LEFT
A wrap-around metallic pot is a fitting match for an equally unusual plant, the Canary Island foxglove (*Isoplexis canariensis*).

selecting pots for plants

MATCHING POTS OF DIFFERING SHAPES, SIZES, AND TEXTURES TO THE RIGHT PLANT FOR THEM IS GREAT FUN.

Get this match-making process right and you will have a pot and plant combination of style and distinction. The fun begins when you start to put the pots and plants together. There are so many plants that grow as well, if not better, in containers than in the greater garden that you can bring every part of the garden into your container collection. Now is the moment to match the shapes, materials, size, and style of pot with the particular plants that suit them to perfection.

It is show time – the moment to set the scene, dress the stage, and produce show-stopping displays using pots and plants that will create different styles and moods. The cast list is as infinite as it would be for the wider garden, but space is usually the factor that limits a container gardener's choices.

Get to know the plants that will give you the best value, so that you can fill the space, however large or small, to maximum effect. Divide your attention between the plants that will give you long-term ornament and those that are short-term with their own seasonal time-line.

Long-haul plants

Herbaceous perennials will give you longer-term rewards in that they survive from year to year for many years, but they die back in winter, so

are in essence not available during their dormant period.

Trees and shrubs that lose their foliage in winter – deciduous plants – may have outstanding autumnal or spring foliage, such as that of Japanese maples, or even coloured stems, such as those of dogwoods.

Evergreen trees or shrubs are probably the most sought-after plants in the container gardener's repertoire. Their glossy green foliage is attractive in all seasons and provides a good foil for the brighter colours of flowering plants. And evergreen is not just green. Within this group of plants there are evergreens with golden leaves, with gold-and-green, cream-to-white-and-green variegations, and silvery leaves.

Seasonal plants

Annuals provide the main colour and excitement in seasonal displays. They don't survive from year to year, so once their flowering season is over, they are removed from container plantings. But in their season, they are among the brightest and most showy plants. There are also annual climbers including sweet peas and black-eyed Susans. Bulbs, although grown from year to year, also provide annual colour, either in spring or summer.

Your potted plant collection can be permanent or seasonal. A seasonal planting usually consists of bulbs and bedding plants that you pot up and enjoy while they are at their best,

ABOVE
Taking the spiky with the smooth. The pointed foliage of *Agave attenuata* seems at home in these rusted-metal containers, whose weathered sides appear to mimic the warm, earthy look of terracotta.

OPPOSITE
Ornamental grasses including *Carex*, *Pennisetum*, and blue grass (*Festuca glauca*) are the perfect subjects for these weathered-copper pots shaped like flower-sellers' buckets.

then replace with the next season's flowering beauties. Permanent collections can be specimen plants, grown for their year-long attractions. Evergreen shrubs and trees are the basis of a permanent collection, with perennials and grasses also coming in and out of the seasonal frame in such a collection.

You can grow collections of spring and summer bulbs, evergreen and deciduous shrubs and trees, as well as stand-alone, specimen trees, such as holly, box, and bay. These three evergreens have the added advantage that they respond well to being shaped into spirals, pyramids, and standards, with mop-heads.

Using vibrant annuals can fire up the colour schemes for spring and summer, while perennials can bring a main framework of colour into play in spring, summer, and autumn.

Roses, especially patio varieties that have been bred to grow well in pots, should also be part of your plant palette. Climbers, such as sweet peas, clematis, and jasmine, will provide focus points at a higher level, while succulents and grasses will add sculptural and highly textured effects to your garden.

OPPOSITE
On summer evenings patios become the focus for entertaining, so lighting is often an important element. Here, the blue uplighting emphasizes the form of the plants, drawing attention to the beautiful pleated leaves of the palm (*Trachycarpus fortunei*) and the frilly grey leaves of *Senecio cineraria* 'White Diamonds'.

RIGHT
Bamboo (*Pseudosasa japonica*) occupies a row of tall cubes, creating a leafy canopy of welcome shade and offering a sense of privacy in a sunny patio garden.

And then there is the vegetable garden: it's perfectly feasible to grow fruit, vegetables, and herbs in containers, so that, even if you don't have the space for a full-size potager garden, you can still cultivate the tastiest plants for your kitchen.

But today's stylish pots look good enough to come into the garden or onto the patio in their own right, without plants. Place these empty pots strategically in the garden or patio, so that their shape can be appreciated. They make their own architectural statement and can be used as focal features in the same way that you might use a piece of statuary or a sundial.

Plants for tall containers

A tall container, or even a container placed on a pedestal, will be an ideal foil for long trailing foliage plants such as ivy, ground ivy (*Glechoma hederacea* 'Variegata'), and *Helichrysum petiolare* 'Limelight', with its softly textured, lime-green leaves, or the grey-green form *Helichrysum petiolare*, and *Plectranthus verticillatus*. Trails of flowering stems of *Lobelia erinus*, ivy-leaved geraniums, and petunias in the Cascade and Surfinia series, and creeping Jenny, with its bright yellow summer flowers, will make an attractive display spilling over from the top of a tall container. Nasturtiums, particularly, *Tropaeolum majus* 'Alaska', with its creamily variegated foliage and orange-yellow flowers, and yellow flowered *Bidens ferulifolia*, are also suited to tall pot displays.

Large plants such as conifers, some ferns, and cacti with deep tap roots will thrive in deep containers.

Lilies need a deep root run for their massed fibrous roots – traditional tall lily pots are known as "long toms". Climbers, grown on triangular obelisks set in the top of tall pots need the extra depth of the pot for aesthetic reasons, as do upright and standard fuchsias.

Deep and wide pots

Pots that are deep and wide are useful for planting formally shaped trees such as standard bays or spiral box. The extra width and depth of the pot allows for the planting of a softening, ground- and pot-covering layer of plants, such as variegated trailing foliage plants with, say, a rim of single-colour, trailing petunias, to offer a festoon of colour at the foot of the shaped tree.

ABOVE
A shallow dish is the perfect shape to show off low-growing succulents such as these echevarias. Any dish will do, as long as it has a hole in the bottom for the free flow of rainwater away from the plant roots, and the compost has added grit for drainage.

OPPOSITE
The dwarf fan palm (*Chamaerops humilis*) creates an architectural focal point. Use a sack-barrow to move it inside to the conservatory, or other indoor space, during the cold winter months.

Provided that the deep pot is stable and won't overbalance in windy conditions, it will be suitable for growing fruit trees in small gardens. Figs, peaches, apples, cherries, and blueberries will all do well in a reasonably large and deep container. Check that the cultivar, in the case of apples and cherries, is on a dwarfing rootstock. Growing the fruit or any other tree in a container will have a dwarfing effect on the plant in any case.

A tall strawberry pot, although designed to be filled with its namesake, will make a good central feature for a herb garden, which essentially has a low-growing character. The pouches in the pot will be useful for clumps of prostrate thyme or trailing rosemary, while the top of the pot will look good with a bushy herb such as lavender or myrtle planted into it.

Wide and shallow pots

Pots that are wide and shallow offer an attractive area for displaying low-growing spring bulbs, alpines, and mat-forming plants.

Ground-huggers or mat-forming plants such as sempervivums (houseleeks), saxifrages, and creeping thymes are well suited to wide, shallow troughs, spreading in mounds and rosettes, as well as in ground-covering mats. Alpine pinks such as *Dianthus alpinus, D. deltoides,* and *D. neglectus*, and thrifts, which form soft foliage mounds, with flower stems rising straight up out of the clump, also grow well in such containers.

Even in a miniature planting of low-growing plants, it is necessary to have a variation in height. Slow growing dwarf conifers, with their upright or dome shapes, will provide the necessary height changes.

Low-growing bulbs such as *Crocus* and *Iris reticulata*, closely planted, and in one colour, offer a jewel-like, treasure-casket effect. Tulips set in a sea of blue forget-me-nots will also provide good spring colour in wide, shallow pots. *Cyclamen coum*, dwarf and species tulips, or multi-flowered tulips, will also be well-suited to wide, low containers.

A group of similar, broad and shallow pots with the same type of plants, such as houseleeks or cacti, arranged on a stone patio, will provide its own textured, chequer-board patterns.

Pots for window-ledges

Window-ledges can be transformed into mini-gardens, holding plants that express the essence of each season, and that will also enhance the facades of your home. Some of the most attractive window-ledge displays are those where the colours are vibrant, and the vigour of the plants create a swirling mass of colour, which completely obscures the container, almost enveloping the window it is dressing.

Use a number of pots on a window-ledge and set them into a long, rectangular water-holding tray, or individual plant saucers. This is

RIGHT
Japanese maple (*Acer palmatum*) is a perfect permanent pot plant. Its tendency is to spread horizontally rather than grow upwards. It offers great visual value from spring until autumn. This one is just taking on its autumn tinge, as its arching branches hang prettily over the edge of a ridged, terracotta pot.

particularly important if you live in a multi-residence property (the neighbours below don't want to be watered too). Since these pots are usually sited high above pavements or front gardens, make sure that they cannot shift off the window-ledge.

Even in the small space of a window-ledge it is possible to create a stunning display. A reduced palette of one colour with foliage plants – for example, a rich red pelargonium with ivy – would provide a vibrant, yet formal style. Cascade and Surfinia petunias, together with lobelia in complementary colours, and trails of fuchsias would suggest a more relaxed, almost country style. Silver and grey is a popular colour combination for foliage in window-ledge plantings. Add a plant with a white variegation in its foliage, such as ivy, or a white-flowered plant, for example white lobelias to create a mini-Sissinghurst effect. In a north-facing site use ivy and box, as well as shade-loving ferns, and cyclamen. In full sun use floriferous diascias in a range of pastel colours.

Tall and wide pots

Large pots offer good proportions and work well with statuesque, architectural plants such as yucca, aloe, melianthus, cordylines, and aeoniums. Because of their size, they can hold sufficient plants to create a dramatic floral effect and can be planted in layers with material that will keep going over several seasons.

Although big pots with narrow tops or wide bellies are attractive, they are not practical for plant growing. The plant roots will follow the curve of the pot, and, if you have to repot the plant, it will be difficult or impossible to remove it without damaging plant or pot. In addition, if waterlogged compost is frozen in the narrow neck of the pot, it will expand against the terracotta, and may damage it, especially if the vessel is not frost-proof. Instead, use the big-bellied or wide-shouldered pots as decorative features in their own right, or as holders for smaller pots, which you can replace when they are past their best with other show-stopping displays.

Place upright, bushy shrubs at the centre of wide, tall pots and smaller varieties around the edges, with trailing plants frothing over the edges to soften the sides of the containers. If the pots themselves are highly decorated, it is best to use them for growing upright plants and leaving the decorated sides visible.

Climbing plants such as black-eyed Susan, cup-and-saucer vine, and even clematis, will look attractive

OPPOSITE
Balancing, as if by magic, shining copper cones stand "on pointed toes" in a gravel garden. They are a perfect match for the dramatic blue-leaved hosta (*Hosta sieboldiana*), which, with its matt, verdigris-like sheen, has a look of ageing copper.

ABOVE
Grow scarlet-flowered, ivy-leaved pelargoniums to heighten the drama of a 17th-century, weathered, terracotta pot.

LEFT
Go geometric with rounded plants, such as box (*Buxus sempervirens*), in an angular, modern, galvanized cube. Regular clipping of the box as it grows will keep it compact.

growing in tall, wide pots, provided that they are given well-proportioned supports. Keep the base of the pot in the shade if possible when growing clematis. Allow the climbing plants to flourish naturally, so that trails of soft foliage and flowers occur at different levels.

You can also put in place canes or obelisks to support the climbers. Train climbing annuals such as sweet peas and black-eyed Susan into pyramid shapes. Because of their depth, large and wide pots are useful for shrubs and for topiarized box and yew shapes. In a formal setting, cover the surface of the compost at the base of the plant with gravel to give a formal finish to the planting.

Wide pots also suit flowing plants such as grasses, and single specimens offer a formal look for a central position, perhaps marking the junction of paths. Although they seem to suit tall architectural plants so well, tall pots can also be used effectively with low growing, closely packed plantings of saxifrage or sempervivums.

Treat your container collection as a continually changing border that rises and falls with colour as the seasons change. However, remember that once a plant stops looking its best, you can either replace it in the planting scheme, or move the whole pot out and bring on a new one to refresh the scene.

ABOVE LEFT
Shallow bowls house a trio of succulent collections. A mulch of gravel on the compost surface reflects heat and prevents excessive evaporation of water.

ABOVE AND OPPOSITE
See what a difference a pot can make. Different phormiums ('Yellow Wave' and 'Maori Chief') offer similar fountain-like effects, but couple them with containers that enhance their colours, and you create strikingly different styles.

choosing the best site

FIND THE RIGHT SITE FOR YOUR POTS AND PLANTS AND THEY WILL THRIVE, PROVIDING YOU WITH BURSTS OF FLOWER COLOUR AND WITH FOLIAGE TEXTURE.

Plants adapt to a wide range of situations where they grow naturally in the wild, and many man-made environments offer similar conditions. Most plants need sunshine and shelter from wind to grow well, but some need more shade than others. And in every site there are areas that offer sun, shelter, and shade in varying degrees.

There are plants to suit the conditions that exist in most sites that favour container gardening, such as patios, courtyards, balconies, basement areas, and roof-top gardens. Each situation has individual conditions: basements are usually shaded, while roof-top gardens and balconies are likely to be windy, with wind-rock and dessication of plants the attendant problems. Roof gardens and balconies may be shaded by other buildings, but equally may be in full sun. And in hot climates shade will be a benefit. Though shaded areas are likely to miss out on rainfall, the pots sited in shade, once watered, will keep moist longer; although watering is essential, it can therefore be less frequent. It's important that you choose plants that can survive these conditions, otherwise you will have stressed-out, unhealthy plants, and there will be little pleasure or beauty in such an outcome.

PREVIOUS PAGE
Two matching pairs of tall, earthenware containers house identical specimens of shapely box plants and stylishly offset the unremitting starkness of a white wall below an espalier pear in a courtyard garden.

ABOVE
Bamboo, although it won't grow to its regular size, needs large containers, and will create a light, screening windbreak for a roof-top garden, enabling you to grow a wider range of plants than in an unsheltered environment.

OPPOSITE
Place containers with fragrant plants such as sweet cherry pie (*Heliotropium arborescens*) on a pathway or near a patio, so that you can enjoy its perfume as day turns to dusk. Its clusters of blue flowers provide colour over a long period in summer.

Sunbathers and shade-lovers

If the site has an open, sunny aspect, you will be able to grow a wide range of plants in pots, especially those that are sun-loving and drought-tolerant. The leaves of some of these sunbathing beauties, many of which originate in Mediterranean climates, are specially adapted to help them save water. Some have slim, often slightly furry, silver foliage, while others, known as succulents, have fleshy leaves that conserve moisture. Depending on how hardy they are, they may need protection in winter.

Spring and summer bulbs and bedding plants thrive in full sun. These plants will provide all the colour you need through the seasons, while permanent plantings of evergreen shrubs and trees are the best choice for the backbone of your all-year container collections.

Areas of shade can be brightened up with pots of spring bulbs, as well as foliage plants with good silver colouring or variegations. Sun-loving perennials, such as *Argyranthemum* 'Chelsea Girl', and annuals, including petunias and lobelias, will thrive in combination with foliage plants when in a sunny position.

If your site faces south, the plants will have a good level of winter light and warmth in summer to promote healthy growth. Sites that are east- or west-facing will be shady in the afternoon or morning, but will have good light at other times to support a container garden. Sites that face north are at a disadvantage as they are likely to be shady all through the year and are colder and damper in winter than other situations.

Windy sites are problematic for most plants, so shelter provided by other items, such as climbers on trellises, or by glass or wooden screens, reduces the impact, and increases the range of plants you can grow. Evergreens, with their strong, leathery leaves, such as spotted laurel (*Aucuba japonica*) and *Euonymus japonicus*, as well as low-growing, mound-forming plants such as busy Lizzie, will be a boon in these conditions. Grasses, with their thin flowing leaves are ideal in windy sites, as they move with the breeze, with little ill effect on the plants.

Shade-lovers, such as ferns and hostas, will brighten the darkest basement, and illuminate dark areas of evergreens in the garden, Clematis, on the other hand, prefer cool shade for the roots to grow well and full sun for good flower development.

Matching backgrounds

Once you have the right plants for the prevailing conditions, think how they will look in situ. You need to match the plants to the background against which they will be placed. Fences, walls, trellis, and even plants, such as evergreens and "evergolds" all offer a foil to colourful flowering plants. The plainer the background, the more attractive the flowering species in the foreground will look.

LEFT
Raised beds support a wide range of plants that enjoy full sun. These include the arching-stemmed *Gaura lindheimeri*, the drought-tolerant *Osteospermum* 'Whirlygig', and the annual tobacco plant (*Nicotiana alata*). Plants that tolerate shade better, including pineapple mint and the black, grass-like *Ophiopogon planiscapus* 'Nigrescens', can be grown in the lee of the wall.

having the right tools

IN ADDITION TO THE POTS, COMPOST, AND PLANTS THAT YOU WILL BE USING, YOU WILL NEED SOME BASIC GARDEN TOOLS TO PLANT, GROOM, WATER, AND TRANSPORT YOUR POTS AND PLANTS.

If you are mixing compost on the grass, the patio, roof terrace, or even on a floor inside your home, a clean plastic ground sheet is essential. A hand trowel is useful for planting and potting up, top-dressing pots, and removing plants from their containers. A hand fork is helpful for loosening weeds and breaking up compacted compost. You may need a spade for filling very large containers with compost.

A pair of strong gardening gloves is a good idea if you are dealing with sharp or rough-edged or moist containers, as well as for mixing compost and pruning roses. Also necessary are a pair of secateurs for pruning and deadheading, and, depending on how many shaped or topiarized plants you have in containers, a pair of hand shears. A garden knife is another useful option for pruning.

A sack trolley or pot castors are necessary for moving large and heavy containers to different sites. If you are using pot castors, it is best to put them in place before you plant up the container and keep them in situ through the life of the container.

Drainage materials include gravel and shards of broken clay pots. If the pot has no drainage holes, you will need a drill to make some.

Watering utensils

A watering can, preferably one that you can use with one hand, is essential. Although watering cans come with "roses" for fine spraying or misting, it is best to remove them so that you can reach into the centre of the container at soil level, rather than wet the leaves. A watering can with a long spout may be better for getting right into the centre of a large pot, but you will need two hands to use it.

If you have a large container collection you may consider a hose more practical, but make sure that you buy one with a multi-purpose rose, so that you can direct the water efficiently. You may also want to have a lance attachment for a hose, if you have to water plants in containers that are situated above ground level on window-ledges or on walls. There are a number of watering systems that can be laid into place to water collections of pots.

A bucket for carrying compost, or for holding water to soak and revive a dried-out plant and compost, is another essential piece of kit for the container gardener. Keep a bucket filled with water as a reservoir, if your pots are far from a water source.

RIGHT
The correct tools will make light of container maintenance. You will need a sack trolley to move containers once they are filled with plants and compost. A hand fork and trowel are the best tools for planting up and removing plants from pots. A watering can, preferably with a long spout, is best for directing water onto the compost and avoids wetting the foliage.

planting, potting-up, and mulching

GIVE YOUR CONTAINER PLANTS A GOOD START WITH BEST-QUALITY COMPOST AND YOU WILL BE REWARDED WITH HEALTHY PLANTS ALL THROUGH THE SEASON.

There are two basic types of compost: soil- or loam-based, and soil-less or multi-purpose. There are also many specialist composts, some formulated for pot plants and bulbs.

Loam- or soil-based composts are heavier than the multi-purpose or container ones, so give weight and stability to the pot. They are easier to re-wet should they dry out, and include nutrients. They are good for permanent plantings of climbers, trees, shrubs, and hardy perennials.

Soil-less composts are usually peat-based, and lighter in weight. They are relatively clean to handle and hold water well, but are difficult to re-wet. You can add water-retaining granules and slow-release fertilisers to the basic compost when you pot up. They are good for seasonal, short-term annuals and bulbs.

Lime-hating or acid-loving plants, including some magnolias, rhododendrons, pieris, and camellias, need special ericaceous composts.

Pots and tools needs to be clean and ready for use. Buy compost as fresh as possible and check that the bag is undamaged. Pots must have drainage holes. Before planting up, soak the plant in its pot in water, so that it doesn't suffer any setback

OPPOSITE
Terracotta pots of all sizes, provided that they are frost-resistant, offer a good environment for plants, because, as they are porous, they "breathe'"and do not waterlog the roots.

ABOVE
The starting point for a successful container collection is the choice of pot. Depending on the size of the pot, you can use it to hold just one large specimen plant, or a collection of plants. Make that sure it has sufficient drainage holes in its base before you plant it up.

RIGHT
A loam-based compost with added grit helps the sun-loving plants *Osteospermum jucundum* and monkey flower (*Mimulus aurantiacus*) to thrive.

when replanted. Soak bare-rooted trees, shrubs, and roses in water for an hour before planting. Soak clay pots before use.

Plants need good drainage. Fill a very large pot with up to one third drainage material, such as crocks, stones, or gravel. Line the base of smaller pots with crocks, covering the drainage hole to prevent compost leaching out when you water.

Half fill the container with compost, add water-retaining gel or granules and slow-release fertilizer. Knock the new plants out of their pots, and, if they are pot-bound, tease out the roots. Set the plants into the new container and fill in the space around them with compost. Firm the compost with your fingers. Continue filling and firming, but leave a 2cm (⁴⁄₅in) gap at the top of the pot, so that you can water the compost without flushing it out of the pot. Firm the compost in place, water the plant well, and add a layer of mulch.

You should stake trees and provide sturdy supports for climbers, as well as for some vegetable crops.

Mulching materials

Mulch offers many practical advantages, preventing water evaporating, and insulating against extreme temperatures.

Gravel is the traditional mulch for containers and is widely available, inexpensive, and durable. Pebbles and cobbles look attractive in large containers holding just one plant. Glass gravel comes in a range of colours; it is expensive, but it is very attractive with alpines and succulents. Chipped bark, available in a range of natural shades, and cocoa shell, are also used as mulches.

ABOVE
If you are using a very large pot for a plant that needs only a small amount of compost, you will need to fill about three-quarters of the pot with crocks or drainage material and only a quarter with compost.

OPPOSITE
The folded young leaves of the fan palm (*Chamaerops humilis*) are a good match for this textured ceramic pot. Finish off with a layer of stones as a water-retentive and decorative surface mulch.

watering, feeding, and pruning

NURTURE YOUR POTTED PLANTS. GIVE THEM WATER, NUTRIENTS, AND A LITTLE TENDER LOVING CARE THROUGH THE YEAR TO KEEP THEM IN PEAK CONDITION.

Compost must not be allowed to dry out completely. Some composts are mixed with water-retaining gel, making water available to the plant over a period of time, thus reducing the need for frequent watering. This is helpful if you are unable to water every day, and if all your containers are filled with the same compost. Otherwise you will have to remember which pots have the gel, and water them less frequently. In winter these composts present problems, as they retain moisture so well that plant roots can rot. Cold, water-logged compost increases the likelihood of pots freezing and breaking.

Water-retaining gel is useful in pots that contain spring and summer bedding that will be removed when finished. You can then also replace the compost with a standard mix.

As a general rule you need to water containers daily in the growing season and more frequently in very warm weather. Saucers placed under pots will act as reservoirs and mulch will reduce the amount of water evaporated from the soil. If small containers dry out in between waterings, leave them standing in water for a couple of hours.

Remove the rose from the watering can and apply the water directly from the spout into the centre of the pot, straight onto the soil,

avoiding the leaves. This way the water goes directly to where it is most needed, the roots, and the leaves will not be scorched.

It is best to water in the evenings or early morning, in the cooler parts of the day. This way the plant absorbs the water before it is evaporated out by the sun.

When you go away on holiday, remember to ask someone to water your plants, or set up an automatic watering system. Don't assume that pot plants do not need water after heavy rain. Dense foliage usually prevents rainwater getting through to the soil. Collecting your own rainwater in a water butt is sensible, and, if you live in a hard-water area, essential for watering lime-hating plants.

ABOVE
Group together sun-loving and drought-tolerant plants, such as palms and agaves. This makes for easier maintenance, as their watering needs are similar.

OPPOSITE
Most compost mixtures have some added fertilizer, but once this is used up, plants need regular feeding during their growing and flowering season.

Feeding

Most composts contain added nutrients sufficient for about six weeks. After this time, you will need to start feeding. Plants need nitrogen for foliage growth, phosphorous for flower development, and potassium, or potash, for ripening fruit and root development, as well as trace elements. You can provide all these with liquid feeds, foliar sprays, and by adding slow-release fertilizer granules to the compost.

Annuals, which have a short, but intense flowering season, need weekly feeding with a liquid tomato feed, as will any other container crops you have. In the case of crops, feed them once flowers begin to form.

Shrubs, trees, roses, climbers, and perennials benefit from a general liquid fertilizer in spring, early, and late summer. Bulbs need a boost after flowering, and poorly growing succulents may need a dose of general fertilizer in spring. Lime-hating plants, such as azaleas, need specialist fertilizer after flowering.

Organic fertilizer in the shape of pellets of chicken manure is a good source of nutrients. You can dissolve it in water to make a liquid feed, or mix it into the compost where it acts as a slow-release fertilizer.

Pruning and general care

Woody plants, flowering shrubs, and climbers need pruning for shape, and to remove any dead or diseased wood. Shape topiarized plants such as box, bay, and holly in late spring, after the last frosts, and again during the year if they grow out of shape.

You need to deadhead annuals and other flowering plants regularly during the flowering season, to keep a steady succession of flowers coming on. I go armed with a pot to hold the spent flower heads and a pair of sharp secateurs or scissors. Sometimes you can nip the dead flowers off using finger and thumb, but it is best to make a clean cut, so that you don't damage the stems.

If permanent container plants become pot-bound you will need to re-pot them into a larger container. When they are mature, and too large to re-pot, you can refresh the compost (this is known as top-dressing) by replacing the top 2–3cm (⅘–1⅕in) with new compost. It may be necessary to root-prune the plant, and re-pot it with fresh compost.

OPPOSITE
Culinary herbs, including mint, marjoram, sage, and thyme, need to be cut back to prevent flowering, as their main culinary use comes from their foliage. Turn the pots round and harvest from different parts of the plants, to keep them in attractive shapes.

BELOW
Box responds well to shaping or topiarizing. Keep this tabletop finish by regular clipping over with a pair of hand-shears.

overwintering

IN WINTER, CONTAINER PLANTS ARE MORE VULNERABLE THAN THOSE THAT GROW IN THE GARDEN SOIL OF YOUR BEDS AND BORDERS.

Tender plants are most at risk, but even those plants that would normally survive winter outdoors, may need protection when they become container plants. Their survival depends on two factors: one is the moisture level and temperature of the compost, and the other is the lowest air temperature that they can adapt to in winter. If compost becomes saturated or waterlogged, the resulting cold and wet is too much for the roots of most plants to contend with.

As far as temperature is concerned, you need to know what the average minimum temperature for your area is, then you can determine which plants can stay outside unprotected over the winter; which will need protection outdoors; and which will need to be brought into some shelter, or even omitted completely from your container gardening.

In winter, remove and store plant saucers so that there is no danger of water collecting and then freezing, which is likely to damage plants and their pots. It is a good idea to put feet under the pots, again preventing the base of the pot from freezing. You can buy these from garden centres. Raising your pots on feet will also improve drainage, so that the plant's roots are not in cold, wet, and clogged soil. In this dormant period err on the side of caution, and reduce watering to a bare minimum. If the rootball becomes saturated the roots will expand if frozen, and the wood is likely to split.

You don't have to have a heated greenhouse to overwinter tender perennials or exotic plants that you grow in containers, but it does help to have some place where you can offer them shelter.

Unless you know that your pots are frost-proof you should always move them into a dry and frost-free site. If they are too large to move, you may need to provide some in-situ insulation. Bubble wrap, horticultural fleece, or hessian sacking are useful "man-made" blankets, but you can also provide protection by packing straw around the pots or by tucking them up with a covering of conifer branches.

In colder areas, exotic plants, which have generally become more affordable and popular in recent times, will need to be well wrapped up if they remain outdoors. They are more likely to survive periods of cold and wet better if they are brought into a frost-free greenhouse. In gentle winters and in mild areas, it may be possible to get some "borderline" plants through the winter, in situ, by covering them with "tents" of insulation material.

Tender summer bulbs, dahlias, and cannas should be brought into a frost-free site for a dormant period. Keep them cool, dry, and in a dark environment.

ABOVE
Cordyline australis can be overwintered in a greenhouse or conservatory or you can tie up the strap-like leaves – rather like furling and closing an umbrella – and cover the whole plant with fleece.

OPPOSITE
Phormium tenax is tough enough to endure the winter outdoors in large pots with good drainage and some shelter, but after a snowstorm brush snow off its foliage.

problem solving

PREVENTION IS ALWAYS BETTER THAN CURE. IF QUALITY DRIVES YOUR PURCHASE OF PLANTS, COMPOST, AND CONTAINERS, AND IN ADDITION YOU PROVIDE YOUR CONTAINER GARDEN WITH REGULAR WATER AND NUTRIENTS, YOUR PLANTS HAVE A GOOD CHANCE OF AVOIDING SOME OF THE PESTS AND DISEASES THAT THREATEN THEM.

The best prevention lies in basic hygiene and the choice of healthy, disease-resistant varieties of plants, grown in good conditions. Always keep the patio or container-garden area clean, depriving slugs and snails of their favourite habitats beneath fallen leaves and other plant debris.

Only use clean pots and fresh compost when you repot and pot up , and make sure that you give your plants regular water and nutrients to promote strong, healthy growth. This reduces the likelihood of producing weak plants, susceptible to disease and pest attacks.

With all the daily tender loving care that you are no doubt lavishing on your container plants, you are bound to catch sight of any pests and notice any signs of disease or stress before they have gone too far.

You may be squeamish about handling insects, but manual control of a low-key attack of caterpillars, slugs, or even aphids is the most effective method. Wear lightweight rubber gloves and pick slugs, snails, and caterpillars off – or squish the aphids between gloved forefinger and thumb!

If your pest infestation is a little more advanced, you will have to call in the cavalry, and either apply the right mainstream spray in the correct dosage, or use an organic remedy that deals with the problem.

Whether using mainstream or organic products, the most important rule is to read the product label carefully and follow the instructions to the letter. Sprays should only be used on cool, calm days, when there is little or no wind. Wait until evening before spraying flowering plants, so that you don't harm any beneficial insects such as bees, and never spray directly onto open blooms.

Avoid getting any spray on yourself, and always wash off any that inadvertently splashes onto your skin. Make sure that you keep the equipment you use clean, and store the sprays in a safe place, inaccessible to children and pets.

Different types of pests

Aphids, such as greenfly and blackfly, are sap-sucking insects. They attack young foliage and stems and, if untreated, will weaken and overwhelm the plant. There are sprays available, organic and mainstream, to combat these pests, and, if you see the attack early, you can remove affected shoots and leaves.

Caterpillars, particularly those of cabbage white butterflies, can strip plants bare of foliage. I always check the undersides of foliage for eggs and remove caterpillars manually.

BELOW
Despite the overcrowded nature of container collections, if you combine plants with similar needs, and provide regular watering, feeding, good compost, and frequent deadheading and grooming, they will thrive, providing you with a highly decorative result.

OPPOSITE
Nasturtiums are popular container plants, providing trailing stems of attractive foliage and colourful flowers, but they are prone to attack from caterpillars and aphids, which may destroy the foliage. Keep a close check on plants, and remove caterpillars manually. Aphids can be sprayed, but badly affected foliage and stems will have to be cut off.

There are sprays that will curb large infestations.

Lily beetle with its bright red back, usually out and about in bright sunshine, is one of the most visible pests, but once you disturb it, it flips onto its back. Since its undersurface is brown, it can disappear on the surface of the compost. I always place one hand under the position of the lily beetle, so that when it falls, I will hopefully be able to catch it before it hits the ground. Lily beetles are bad news for lilies and fritillaries, including crown imperials and *Fritillaria pyrenaica*. The adults lay eggs on the plants, which develop into greedy larvae that completely overwhelm the plant. The egg clusters are messy, and you should wear gloves if you squash them.

Slugs and snails are high-profile pests, but they are relatively easy to detect and control: look for nibbled leaves or a slime trail on the compost. In the mainstream corner, bird-friendly slug pellets are available. There is also a biological control using nematodes, which can be watered into the soil; this is effective for six weeks, but won't curb snails. If you raise your pots off the ground on pot feet, it makes it harder for slugs and snails to start the climb up the side.

Preventative measures

If you have birds, hedgehogs, frogs, and toads in the garden, and you keep debris under control, you are less likely to be troubled by slugs and snails. A gravel or cocoa-shell mulch on the surface of the soil will act as a deterrent. Copper rings around the necks of plants, as well as copper tape around the rims of pots, and other barriers, such as cloches to protect

OPPOSITE
Crown imperials flower in spring and are often the first host plants in the season to the bright red lily beetles, which, if left, will decimate lilies and fritillaries. Check the plants daily in sunny weather for any signs of the beetles.

BELOW
When you plant up newly bought spring bedding plants, such as *Primula* 'Jessica', always check the compost for signs of the small, white grubs of the vine weevil. If these pests are caught early, a specific insecticide can be used to soak the compost and kill them. If left, they will damage and ultimately destroy the plants.

young plants, are popular methods of control. Picking slugs off plants in the early evening is a therapeutic pastime for many pot-plant gardeners!

Vine weevil grubs live in compost and eat the roots of plants, causing devastating collapse and death of container plants. Keep an eye out for these small white grubs in the compost when you are potting up containers. Remove and squash them. If you see adult vine weevils on the surface of the soil or notice that something is taking chunks out of foliage, then you are bound to have grubs in the soil. Crush the adults when you see them. You can also use

a biological control based on nematodes, which is watered into the compost in spring or late summer. Some composts come with this control in the mixture. It is not yet available for use with edible container plants, so avoid it in containers that you plan to use for growing fruit, vegetables, and herbs.

Containers plants, growing in such close proximity to each other, are prone to fungal diseases such as powdery mildew, grey mould, and rust. Treat by removing diseased parts of the plant, destroying badly affected examples, and using fungicides as per the manufacturer's instructions.

spring

Enjoy the fresh sparkle of spring as evergreen foliage plants and vibrant bulbs – the fruits of your autumn and winter plantings – become the mainstays of the season, brightening up your containers. Now is the time to plan for the container combinations that will dazzle in summer.

After what often seems to be such a long sequence of grey, snowy, frosty, or wet winter days, there is a fast rush of colour in spring. It feels as if it is a long time coming, then seems to come all at once, when the weather finally settles down. The clear, strong colours of snowdrops, daffodils, tulips, hyacinths, pansies, polyanthas, cowslips, and crocus stand out sharply, and warm the scene, as if reflecting light back to the sun.

Permanent container plants such as flowering shrubs, including rhododendrons and camellias, offer their welcome spring flowers, while deciduous trees and shrubs, including Japanese maples, leaf up, bringing with them the promise of more spectacular tones in autumn.

Spring is a busy time in the garden, and it is no different in the container garden. Apart from admiring and enjoying the wonderful pots that are colouring up daily, the gardener has to plan to make to ensure that the rest of the year is as exciting. There are permanent plantings to tidy up and prepare for their growing season, new containers to plan, seeds to sow and new plants to buy and plant up.

Local weather, time, and space are the main factors that will decide how much you can get done each day. Plants are particularly vulnerable, as they are ready to burst into growth whenever there is a warm spell, and it is these fresh shoots that are at risk if the weather then turns cold. In frosty periods don't overwater, as this leads to water-logged compost, which may freeze and damage plant roots.

Seeds and plug plants

Depending on how mild the spring is you can sow seeds of annuals ready for displays later in the season. Sow half-hardy annuals indoors or in greenhouses, and hardy annuals outdoors in the growing site, if local conditions permit. Once all danger of frost is gone, you can plant out the half-hardy annuals into their growing positions.

If you have the time and the necessary facilities or indoor space, it is very satisfying to grow your own new plants from seed. If not, wait until late spring or early summer, and

PREVIOUS PAGE
Repetition of pots holding the same plants provides a satisfying continuity of colour and offers a border-like effect in a small space.

OPPOSITE
Hyacinths are a great choice for front gardens in the spring – their scent welcomes visitors to your door. There are so many colours to choose from, including blue, pink, deep red, and glowing white, to brighten up the darkest season.

RIGHT
Perky, spring-flowering cowslips team well with the simplicity of the painted metal containers. When they stop flowering replace them with fresh plants.

buy into the "young-" or "plug-" plant revolution. There has been a steady increase in the range of ornamental and edible plants that you can buy from garden centres and nurseries, or order from seed companies, as small seedlings or plug plants. Late winter is the last chance for orders from seed companies, which normally deliver in early and late spring.

Remember that the plants you buy from garden centres, DIY sheds, or nurseries are likely to have just come out of warm shelter. Once they come into your care they will need to be hardened off and accustomed gradually to the outside conditions.

Plug plants are relatively expensive compared to growing your own seedlings, but well worth it in terms of time, effort, and space, especially if you don't have a greenhouse. Plug plants come ready to be potted up, but won't need house room for long. Although they are dearer, you are unlikely to waste any of the plants, as you would if you grew too many of your own seedlings.

OPPOSITE
A wide bowl offers space for a good-sized clump of dark *Tulipa* 'Queen of the Night', nestling in a bed of pale pansies. The pansies will probably outlive the tulips, so remove the bulbs when they fade. Re-pot the bulbs and keep them fed and watered, so that they can make the embryonic flowers for the next year.

ABOVE LEFT
Repeated plantings make a bold statement on a paved area, helping to break up a plain and boring surface.

LEFT
A dark doorway is brought to life by these bright-pink anemones. Choose plants with dark foliage, such as heuchera, to make the pink stand out even more.

Spring bulbs

At this time of year your containers will be fizzing with colour from spring-flowering bulbs, variegated and evergreen plants, and spring-flowering plants such as primulas, pansies, and camellias.

Rising ground temperatures and the warmth and light of spring sunshine is the spur that bulbs in containers need to burst out of their buds and display their colourful flowers. Daffodils, in a wide range of sunny tones from bright yellow through to cream and apricot, are the most popular choice for containers.

There are so many bulbs to choose from, but using a single type per container results in a better overall look to the planting, and you can be sure that they will all flower together. This also means that once the flowering period is over you can simply remove the bulb pots from the container site and allow them to die down out of sight.

LEFT
Underplant narcissus with white *Bellis* daisies to make a fresh spring combination for a modern, metal container.

ABOVE
Gorgeously scented, paper-white narcissus contrasts in colour and form with deep-blue grape hyacinths.

OPPOSITE
Disguise and soften the bare stems of upright plants, for example these dramatic purple ornamental kales, by planting an understorey of clump-forming plants such as hyacinths and primulas.

You can also plant them in tiers or layers so that you can pack more into the pots. The highest layer must be planted to the minimum depth required (roughly three times the size of the bulb), and and lower layers can be planted deeper. They will all flower at roughly the same time, and provide a full and flower-packed punch.

I prefer to grow bulbs in single varieties or species in small pots that I drop into spaces in larger containers, just as the bulbs are beginning to flower. Then, when they have finished flowering, I remove them, pot and all, from the main container and replace them with new bulbs or other flowering plants as the season changes. If you don't have the space to grow your own plant inserts, you will find that garden centres are filled with an array of bulbs in pots that can be used in this way for instant and short-term effects.

In spring, with tulips, daffodils, crocus, and other flowering spring bulbs providing such masses of colour, you will be reaping the benefit of your autumn plantings. Mid-spring is the time to start thinking about planting bulbs of cascading tuberous begonias and other summer-flowering bulbs. Keep them in shelter until all danger of frost has passed. Only then plant them out

LEFT
Take into consideration the colours of existing features, such as this blue table, to inspire your colour choice for pots and plants when planning your spring bulb collections.

OPPOSITE
Think colour in spring and really go for it! Splash out with orange pots as a base for the bold flowers of *Tulipa* 'Hermitage' underplanted with red *Bellis* daisies.

Pots are perfect for growing plants with soil preferences: some "fuss pots" thrive in an acid or lime-free soil. It is easy to give these "lime-haters" or "acid-loving" plants, such as camellias, rhododendrons, and some Japanese maples, the neutral-to-acid conditions they prefer.

Clockwise from above: *Camellia japonica* 'Lavinia Maggi';
Rhododendron 'Bow Bells'; and Japanese maple.

into their growing sites. Wallflowers and forget-me-nots are traditional companions for spring bulbs. Plant them up in autumn when you start to plant up your bulb collections, and they will be ready to provide a good base for the bulbs in spring.

Trees and shrubs

Evergreens and conifers provide the backbone of many permanent container-planting combinations throughout the year and are particularly important in spring. Their foliage is usually the main attraction, offering solid greens as well as creamy and golden variegations, which enliven containers when seasonal and deciduous plants have ceased to be ornamental. There are also many evergreens, such as skimmia (*Skimmia japonica*), and a huge range of camellias that offer flowers in spring, and, in the case of skimmia, berries in autumn.

Spring is the time to pay attention to the care of well-established and mature permanent plantings of evergreen trees and shrubs, as well as conifers. If they are overwintering in sheltered sites, make sure that their compost has not dried out, but don't over-water. Roses need to be pruned before they start to make new growth.

This is also the time to look at deciduous trees and shrubs and prune out any dead, damaged, or diseased branches and stems, and to shape, if necessary. Don't do this, though, if a frost is forecast, as the cut shoots can be further damaged.

If trees, shrubs, roses, and conifers have been growing in containers for a while, their compost will need refreshing. Add a deep layer of compost as a top-dressing for these

plants. If they are pot-bound, transplant them into larger pots. Re-pot with fresh compost and added slow-release fertilizer.

If pot-bound plants are already growing in the largest container you have, you will need to root-prune the plants. This means reducing the size of the roots by pruning them with secateurs or a pruning saw. When re-potted they will need fresh compost and regular feeding and watering.

From mid-spring onwards you can plant up newly bought evergreens and conifers, provided it isn't frosty, and the compost is not frozen or too wet. By late spring, when you have completed top-dressing and planting up, it is worthwhile starting to offer these permanent plants additional nutrients in the shape of liquid feeds.

Caring for your perennials

If perennials (herbaceous plants that grow from year to year, some dying

OPPOSITE
Find a postion on the patio, such as on a table or shelf, that will present the flowers of snakeshead fritillary (*Fritillaria meleagris*) at eye-level, so that you can admire their chequer-board patterning at close quarters.

BELOW
Be brave with spring colour combinations – they are only temporary after all – since the most surprising ones can be successful. Here, a gleaming, glazed turquoise pot makes a bold contrast with the bright-pink hyacinth 'Splendid Cornelia'.

back in winter) have filled out, and large clumps have developed in pots, now is the best time to take them out and divide them. Perennials that have been in pots for a number of years will benefit from top-dressing with fresh compost. Towards the end of spring, make a start with a regular feeding programme for all established herbaceous perennial plants.

In late spring, if weather permits, bring succulents and cacti (these are drought-tolerant plants that store water in their leaves) outdoors after their indoor sojourn during winter.

Divide and re-pot clumps of overcrowded sedums and sempervivums, and increase watering frequency. Start feeding them with a small amount of tomato fertilizer during the growing season.

Perennial climbers such as clematis start to shoot rapidly in spring, and these young shoots need to be encouraged to twine around their supports. In late spring you can bed out young plants of cup and saucer vine, as well as Chilean glory vine. You can also begin feeding climbers, as they start to shoot well in spring.

It is a good idea to check the state of canes and other supports for climbing and tall-growing plants that need staking.

Preparing for crop plants

If you are planning to grow vegetables in containers you can either start sowing tomato, pepper, courgette, lettuce, and cucumber seeds indoors in warmth, so that they will be ready to plant out later in the spring or in early summer, depending on weather conditions. In late spring you can sow runner and French beans, as well as pea seeds to plant out in early summer. Home-grown potatoes are among the garden's real treats, and you can grow smaller quantities successfully in pots or in special potato barrels or towers, available from seed companies.

Check that all dead, damaged, and diseased wood is pruned out of fruit trees, apply a top-dressing of a slow-release fertilizer to the compost, and begin to water it more frequently. If you are growing lemon or orange trees in containers, keep them in frost-free sites until the risk of frost is past, then take them outdoors, and start them on a programme of liquid feeding with specialist fertilizers. Citrus plants will grow best in acid composts.

Blueberries need an acid soil, so are good for growing in containers, where you can provide an ericaceous or peat-based compost. 'Earliblue', 'Toro', and 'Brigitta' are varieties that offer delicious fruit in early, mid-, and late summer, respectively. In addition, their foliage turns russet and pink in autumn before it falls. Feed blueberries with sequestered iron.

There are several types of apple bred on dwarfing root stock, so they are suitable for growing in containers. They have an upright, column-like shape.

Perennial herb-garden plants that do well in containers, such as rosemary, thyme, sage, and bay, will also benefit from a top-dressing of slow-release fertilizers. Make spring sowings of herbs such as parsley and marjoram. Unless you live in a sun-baked Mediterranean climate, seeds of basil, my particular "must-have" herb, will have to be sown in the warmth of the indoors.

OPPOSITE
This low-growing ornamental onion (*Allium karataviense*) deserves a place where its intriguing form and texture can be admired at close range.

ABOVE
Colour-matching your plants with their containers helps to make a bold statement, as here, where the pink glow of the blooms of *Rhododendron* 'Madame van Hecke' are picked up in the warm glaze of its pot. Likewise, *Ceanothus* 'Centennial' is just right for this blue-glazed pot.

RIGHT
It is not just the colour, but also the style that you should consider when choosing pots for particular plants. A rustic, woven-twig cache pot for a cluster of daffodils evokes the woodland in spring.

spot colour

plants
- *Nemesia* 'Nebula Mixed'
- *Viola* x *wittrockiana* (pansies)
- *Echeveria glauca*

plant alternatives
- *Tropaeoleum majus* (nasturtium)
- *Salpiglossis sinuata*
- *Lavatera trimestris*
- *Pelargonium* 'Lord Bute'
- *Lobelia erinus*
- *Phlox drummondii* 'Crème Bruleé'
- *Scaevola aemula* 'Blue Wonder'
- *Zaluzianskya capensis* (Cape night phlox)

MATERIALS
- Terracotta containers
- Drainage material (crocks, polystyrene, gravel)
- Loam-based compost
- Colourful cache pot (to hold an inner pot)

Keep the colour flowing from late spring through to summer by sowing or buying bedding plants in succession. You can add to the colour by using eye-catching cache pots to highlight the flowers of a particular planting, but don't go overboard, or you will detract from the overall look of the plant collection.

Late-sown, spring-flowering pansies, such as this mauve collection, will provide strong blocks of single colours in contrast to the mixed colours of the orange, yellow, and red nemesias. You can buy pansies that will flower through the winter, or buy young plants in spring. Sow another lot of nemesias in each month during spring, so that you have waves of plants to bring into position when needed.

Keep the plants in flower by deadheading them as each flower cluster or single flower fades. The plants will keep on producing more flower stems, but once their foliage starts to look stressed, it is time to bring on another whole pot to replace them.

Annual spring and summer bedding plants need full sun. As they are growing in pots, you need to keep them watered and fed, but not drenched. Don't let the compost dry out, as that will stress the plants.

When all danger of frost has passed, you can bridge any flowering gaps with stand-alone tender or conservatory plants, such as the fleshy-leaved succulents including *Echeveria glauca*. Its flowers are pretty, but it is the rosettes of grey foliage that provide a rich contrast to the riot of flower colour in the container. Echeveria, like all succulents and cacti, stores its own water in its leaves, so don't overwater it. When the flowers are spent, remove their flowering stems. Echeverias and other succulents will benefit from being outdoors in summer. Return echeverias to the greenhouse, window-sill, or conservatory at the end of summer, as they are tender plants and will not survive frosts.

To keep the colour going into early summer, there are any number of alternatives. *Salpiglossis* offers similar colour tones to *nemesia* but with larger flowers, while plants such as *scaevola* provide a mass of blue flowers. For perfume there is nothing to beat the Cape night phlox, but only plant it out when all risk of frost has passed. *Nasturtium*, with its scrambling habit, will wind through the pot collection, knitting it all together. There are so many different-coloured nasturtiums available to grow from seed. Make your colour choices based on the other plants and the colour of the cache pot.

Foliage and flowers

plants
- *Skimmia japonica* 'Rubella' (male and female plants)
- *Heuchera* cultivars
- Pansy
- *Hedera helix* 'Glacier'

plant alternatives
- *Choisya ternata*
- *Petunia* 'Tumble Tunes'
- *Plectranthus madagascariensis* (variegated mintleaf)
- *Tellima* cultivars
- *Heucherella* cultivars
- *Helichrysum petiolare*

MATERIALS
- Terracotta pot
- Drainage materials (crocks, polystyrene, gravel)
- Multi-purpose compost
- Added grit for a more open, better-drained medium

Use the evergreen and variegated foliage of permanent plantings to combine with seasonal flowering plants for semi-permanent designs that provide colour, fragrance, and shape through several seasons. The soft, rosy tones of the blousy, open-faced pansies contrast with the clusters of tiny, fragrant flowers of the evergreen shrub, *Skimmia japonica* 'Rubella'. Together they complement the warmth of the traditional terracotta pot.

Put the main plant – the evergreen skimmia – in the centre of the pot, then place a ring of pansies around it, alternating with heuchera plants. Set several ivies into the compost around the rim, to finish the edge of the planting.

Evergreen plants, whether they are plain green, or have mottled or variegated colourings in green and gold or cream and green are invaluable plants for containers. Evergreen foliage is usually smooth and shiny and makes an attractive foil for colourful flowers. Here, the dark green leaves seem to deepen and darken the rich reds of the pansies and the rosy-white flowers of the skimmia, while the heuchera foliage, available in a range of chocolate-bronze and purple tones, offers a regal finish to the collection.

This skimmia is a male form; if you also grow a female plant in the container label it so you know it is the female. The presence of the male plant will ensure that it produces wonderfully red berries in autumn that will last into winter. In winter, male plants begin to produce clusters of pink bobble-like buds, ready to open in spring. Winter-flowering pansies can be replaced in late spring with summer bedding plants such as the rosy red form of *Petunia* 'Tumble Tunes'.

Trailing plants, such as ivy, soften the edges of the planting and make the link between the plants and the container. There are numerous trailing plants that can be used, but ivies, because of the huge variety of colour and shape to the foliage, are the most popular and basic choice. They are hard-working and easy to grow. For a variegated alternative, choose the white and green mintleaf, or, for a silver effect, use *Helichrysum petiolare*.

In spring, when you are replacing the pansies with the next season's bedding plants, top-dress the compost with a mix that contains slow-release fertilizer to provide nutrients. Water the new plants in well, and deadhead flowers once they have faded. Don't deadhead the flowers of female skimmias, or you will deprive yourself of berries in autumn.

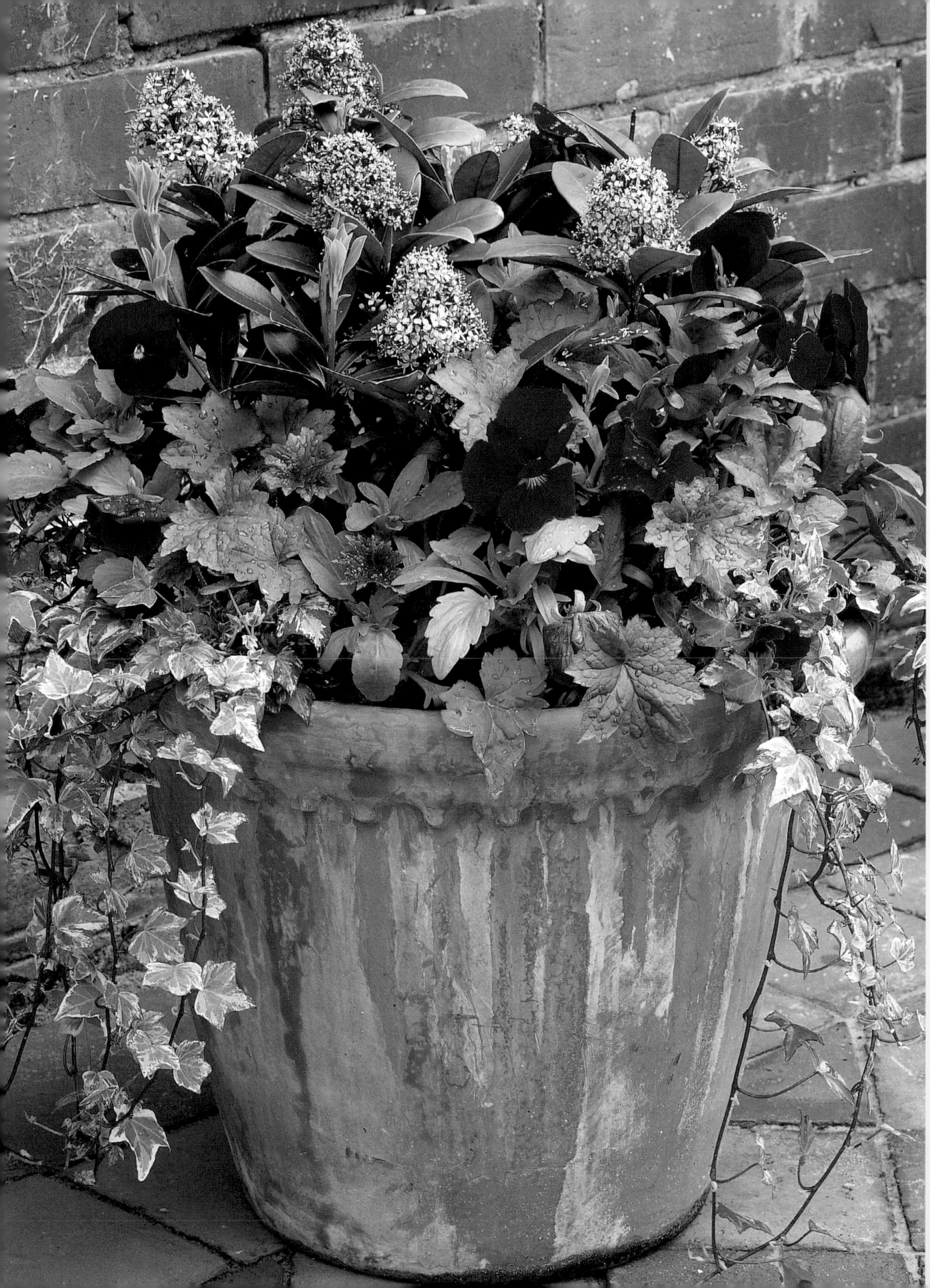

early summer

INSTANT COLOUR IS THE HALLMARK OF THE SEASON. THIS COMES FROM FLOWERS THAT WILL BLOSSOM RELIABLY AND ABUNDANTLY THROUGH THE SUMMER, WITH A LITTLE HELP FROM WATER AND NUTRIENTS. THESE COLOUR-PACKED, SEASONAL "BEDDING" PLANTS PROVIDE AN EVER-RISING TIDE OF CHANGING COLOUR TO ENLIVEN YOUR PLANTINGS.

In early summer, everything starts swarming into growth at the same time. But the weather can still be a bit uncertain, so judgments about sowing directly into the container and planting out half-hardy and tender plants are critical. You can, of course, cover vulnerable plants with fleece in the short term. But in the main, early summer is a delightful time in the container garden.

Perennial plants such as sweetly perfumed dianthus will begin to make their colourful presence felt, and permanent plantings of specimen trees, including Japanese maple, will come into leaf with their fresh new spring colours. These permanent and perennial plants will need regular feeding and watering to keep them healthy and growing well.

As the season goes on, your spring bulbs will be at their lowest ebb, and it is time to take them offstage. A foliar feed will re-energize and prepare them for next year's flowers.

Looking after your lilies

Now is the time to turn your attention to the shoots and stems of any lilies that you planted in autumn. You can also plant lilies from late winter through to early summer. Have several pots planted up, and you will be sure of short-lived but wonderful perfume and sumptuous flowers from early summer through to late summer. Regal lily (*Lilium regale*), with its creamy white blooms and purple markings on the buds, offers its perfumed flowers in early-to-late summer. Highly perfumed Oriental lilies that flower in late summer, including 'Casa Blanca' and 'Star Gazer', are popular choices.

Plant lilies in loam-based compost with added grit or sharp sand to improve the drainage. Place a handful

LEFT
Make sure that you have plenty of plants that pack a double impact of fragrance and colour in early summer, such as *Dianthus* 'India Star', and position the container close to a seating area on the patio.

OPPOSITE
Japanese maple (*Acer palmatum*) offers its fresh green foliage in spring and early summer, and in autumn provides bright yellow hues as it ages.

of grit under the bulbs to keep them from rotting. Plant them into deep pots, so that the bulbs are at least 7–10cm (2⅘–4in) below the surface of the compost. Place the pots in full sun and don't let the compost dry out during the growing and flowering season. Feed them with a dose of general-purpose fertilizer every fortnight during the summer.

At this stage, in early summer, those planted first will be making good progress, and although not yet in flower, the foliage and buds are likely to be under attack from the bright-red lily beetle. The beetles come out in the sun, so you need to check the plants daily, in sunshine. If you don't control these, either by picking them off manually and squashing them, or by spraying with a specially formulated insecticide, the beetles and their offspring will decimate the lilies, leaving you with nothing to enjoy in mid- and late summer.

Bedding plants

The heart of early and late summer colour in pots comes from plants that are known commercially and collectively as annual or summer bedding plants. They are available everywhere. Some are sold with coloured labels so you can pick and mix the colour scheme as you shop.

Depending on their main attraction, whether their flowers, foliage, or scent, this will help to make a strong impact in any setting. Once planted up they are on a mission to flower, and, provided that they are healthy plants, growing in fresh compost, with fertilizer and water provided by you, there'll be no stopping them. Deadhead to keep the flowers coming.

There are several ways to use bedding plants. You can use them *en masse* as the seasonal rainbow-makers in your container collection; select from the huge range and use them to supplement the permanent plantings. You can go for monochromatic colour schemes, ringing the changes as often as you please and your wallet allows.

If you are using bedding plants in this supplementary role, you can move them into an existing planting plan, then remove them when they are past their best. Replace them with something else that will bridge the gap into the next season.

If you are using them as the main attraction, choose the colour scheme you want and find in this group all the plants that fit the bill for the

OPPOSITE
Regal lilies (*Lilium regale*) offer swoon-inducing perfume in summer. Check the plants daily in sunny weather for signs of the dastardly red lily beetle.

BELOW
For cascades of soft, feathery, grey foliage, and bright-yellow and orange-tipped flowers, choose *Lotus maculatus* to dress a sunny window-sill from early summer to late in the season.

front, middle, and/or back of the pot, for draping round the rim, and climbing skywards.

At one time, ivy, whether green, golden or variegated, was almost the only choice as a trailing plant to soften the edges of plantings. Now there is a much wider range of trailing plants, including the tender silver foliage plant *Dichondra argentea* 'Silver Falls', which, at a quick glance, might be mistaken for a cascading splash of cool water.

Another exciting plant that fulfils a similar role is the tender sweet potato vine (*Ipomea batatas*). There are two colours available: purple and citrine-gold. Both are equally dramatic when paired with the right colour combinations.

Cascades of colour

Flowering plants that trail or cascade over the pot rim are high on the list of choices for early and late summer containers. When leafing through seed and plant catalogues look for those plants noted as cascading, and put them on your must-have list.

Trailing pelargoniums are possibly the number one in the hit parade of cascading flowering plants. They have flowers that appear to dance in the light, and, depending on variety, also have attractive foliage. The ivy-leaved pelargoniums, some plain green and others variegated, look very similar to ivy, but have the added bonus of attractive flowers.

Other cascading stars include a fiery orange begonia, 'Bonfire', with masses of pendulous, tubular flowers, combined with attractive, serrated, narrow leaves; and trailing verbenas in a wonderful range of colour, including a mottled blue and

white form, 'Purple Twinkle'. Look out for Tapien verbenas in the plug or small plant catalogues; they make a stunning display, shimmering in the air on a hot day.

Another stunner is the tender lotus plant, *Lotus maculatus*, with its feathery grey-green foliage and pointed, claw-like tawny orange blooms. It offers flowers from early to late summer.

Although I would be tempted to call them standard bedding plants, petunias are available in such an amazing array of colours and are so floriferous, that they must be counted as stars of the container scene. They are usually known by the series name given to them by their originators. So search out the Surfinias, Wave, and Mirage series, which grow to form mounds, with abundant flowers.

Then there are smaller-flowered, cascading, petunia-like flowers, such as *Calibrachoa* 'Million Bells', with zillions of small flowers in tawny and ochre shades. Large, showy, double petunias can be used almost as single subjects in containers. They may need deadheading, but some forms are "self-cleaning", shedding their spent flowers before you need to get your hands sticky as you remove them manually.

Repeating identical plantings gives a cohesive look to any design or plan in the container garden. Provided that they are not caught by frosts, early-flowering campanulas, such as the double-flowered *Campanula* 'Bali', go on for a long time through into late summer, offering delicate, rose-like blooms. Team them up with pots of blue that match the colour of their flowers.

On your basic, standard list for early and late summer floral effects are lobelia, snapdragons, *Bellis* daisies, pansies, impatiens, French or African marigolds, and nasturtiums. You can also sow seeds of hardy annuals, such as dwarf sunflowers, direct into their growing pots, and by midsummer you will have flowers.

But you can go way beyond the basic with plants such as diascia,

arctotis, sanvitalia, and osteospermum. You may be able to grow these on from year to year if you can protect them from frosts, or if you take cuttings and keep the new plants in frost-free conditions over winter.

If you have ordered them as young or plug plants from seed companies, they will arrive in early summer, ready to plant out. However, it is wise to acclimatize or "harden them off" to the outside conditions over a period of days, as they will have been produced in the protective environment of a greenhouse.

Care and maintenance

As the weather warms up, watering is the order of the day, as is a regular feeding programme. I like to water in the evening or early in the day. This regularity also gives you the chance to observe progress and change, and, if there are any pest or disease problems, you can attend to them quickly. Even if there is rainfall during this period, continue to check the plants out, as rainwater tends to run off the leaves, and if the container is filling out well, it is likely that the rainwater won't even touch the soil

BELOW
In early summer you may be able to buy young sunflower plants for instant colour, but you can also sow seeds of the dwarf sunflower 'Baby Face' from early to late spring in pots, and have flowers from early summer through to autumn.

OPPOSITE
Flower power in containers is important, but don't neglect the wonderful effects that you can achieve by combining elegant flowers with dramatic foliage plants, such as phormium, scented pelargonium, and salvia.

For low-maintenance pots choose fleshy-leaved succculent plants – they thrive on neglect and desert conditions! But you must ensure that rainwater can always drain away from the hole in the bottom of the pot, since such plants hate being waterlogged for any length of time.

Clockwise from above: Grey-leaved *Sedum spathulifolium*;
houseleeks (*Sempervivum* species); and *Sempervivum calcareum*.

ABOVE
Bamboos, such as *Fargesia murielae* 'Simba', would normally spread to form a large clump in a garden; in containers, their growth is restricted. They are useful to create an oriental atmosphere in a gravel garden, especially if you choose a suitably decorated pot.

OPPOSITE
Terracotta drainpipes might seem an unlikely choice for a pot. But here they raise the height of the plants, and offer a variation in levels. When the dianthus are over, you can replace them with small pots of seasonal plants.

at all. If pots are standing in saucers or cache pots, make sure that these don't fill up with rainwater, as this would overwhelm young plants.

Watering restrictions are a seasonal hazard for all gardeners, so save as much water as you can in rain butts and use cooled "grey" water recycled from the house, if necessary. Avoid water that contains powerful bio-detergents.

If the heat is too much for some plants, they will begin to wilt. If they can easily be lifted, move them into the shade for the duration of the heat wave, and bring Mediterranean sun-lovers such as lavender and rosemary into the sunny spot. Succulent plants and cacti, including the statuesque agave and aloe plants, are tender and will need protection from frost in winter, but in summer they fall into the category of easy-to-maintain container plants. They are sun-lovers, and as they store water in their specially adapted leaves and stems, they can also be classed as drought-tolerant plants, and can cope with any amount of sun.

Climbers in containers

Climbing plants such as passion flowers and clematis start to take off on their upward journey in early summer. They are extremely useful for adding ornamental interest at different levels to a collection of containers. There are a number of climbers that you can use to provide variation in height. Annual plants that are particularly suited to container collections include nasturtiums, sweet peas, black-eyed Susan, morning glory, and the wonderfully coloured *Ipomea lobata*. Keep climbing plants well watered, and feed them weekly from early summer onwards with a high-potash, liquid-tomato feed. To keep a succession of flowers coming on, deadhead the spent flowerheads of annuals regularly.

In early summer, while perennials and climbers are settling down and establishing, it is a good idea to put in place any stakes and supports that they might need to keep upright in their pots. Take care not to disturb roots as you push canes into the soil,

nor to damage young stems as you tie them onto supports. Use soft twine so that you don't crush the stems.

Foliage and vegetables

The dazzle factor on offer from bedding plants, perennials, and climbers, is high from early through to late summer. But don't neglect the wonderful range of foliage plants that will provide colour and texture in their own right, as well as complement and enhance mixed plantings. Scented pelargoniums often have wonderfully marked foliage, and it is surprising how much variety there can be in a collection of primarily green-coloured plants. Grown for its foliage and stems, bamboo is another plant that suits containers, as some types of it can be invasive in the garden. Some bamboos have green canes, others yellow, and some dark brown to black stems. They need deep pots and grow well in a relatively cool site. They need copious water throughout the growing season, especially in dry, windy weather.

The range of vegetable plants that you can order as young or plug plants is increasing, so you can either grow from seed or use the fast-track way via ready-to-plant plugs. Some crops don't grow as well in containers as they do in the ground, and, of course, depending on how close to the patio and house they are, you may also want an element of ornament as well as productivity. French and runner beans are among my favourites for their crops, which can be green, purple, or yellow podded, as well as for their delicate flowers. Courgettes will take up more space, but a golden-yellow fruited form offers ornament as well as taste. Peppers and aubergines need the sunniest site possible; in very cold areas, you may have to settle for growing them in the greenhouse. Cordon tomatoes need to be staked, but bushy and tumbling plants can be allowed to make their own shapes. Plant them out when all danger of frost is past.

Carrots offer ferny foliage, and will be ready for cropping in early summer. Sow seeds of lettuce in late spring, and keep on sowing into fresh pots, so that you have a succession of leafy salads (see project, pp 94–5). Potatoes are a delight picked from your own pots, although they are not high in the ranks of ornamental plants. All vegetables grown in containers need careful and regular watering and feeding to produce satisfactory crops.

Looking ahead

Deadhead camellias as the flowers fade in order to preserve the plant's energy, and to remove spent flowers that will soon resemble soggy tissues. Camellias need a little extra care in summer. Either top-dress them with a mixture of fresh compost and slow-release fertilizer granules, or apply a balanced liquid feed with sequestered iron. Keep the camellia in a shady site during summer, and make sure that it is well watered as it forms next year's flowerbuds in the summer. If the buds fall, the usual cause is lack of water. When camellias are in flower from late winter into spring, they need to be kept out of any frost pockets, preferably in a site where they can benefit from the warmth of the afternoon sun.

OPPOSITE AND ABOVE
It is possible to use the same plant or forms of a plant to create different styles. Statuesque succulents, such as *Agave americana*, have a role to play as architectural specimens. You can use them in identical, repeated plantings on their own to create an urban-chic look. Alternatively (as above), feature the variegated form *A. americana* 'Marginata' in combination with a brightly coloured trailing plant such as verbena, to achieve a softer, cottage-garden look.

kitchen-garden pots

plants
- Loose-leaf lettuces
- *Tropaeoleum majus* (nasturtium)
- *Beet* 'Bull's Blood'

plant alternatives
- Salad leaf mixtures
- Oriental leaf mixtures

MATERIALS
- Pots or wire baskets
- Plastic lining with holes made in it for drainage, or a layer of coir matting
- Cylindrical chimney pots
- Plug plants or home-raised seedlings
- Multi-purpose compost
- Water-retaining gel
- Drainage material (crocks, polystyrene, gravel)

A container garden is no bar to a vegetable garden. Space may be at a premium, but you can still grow your favourites herbs, salad leaves, and many other vegetables, including beans, peppers, tomatoes, and potatoes. You can also grow fruit, such as strawberries, blueberries, apples, nectarines, and peaches in pots.

Seed companies sell mixtures of salad leaves that are known as "cut-and-come-again" crops, which you can harvest leaf by leaf. They are particularly useful for containers. Sow directly into the pot, or buy them as plug plants and put them straight in.

If you are using a basket, line it with a layer of plastic with drainage holes in it, or use a layer of coir matting. Add some water-retaining gel or granules to improve the water-holding capacity of the compost, and add a layer of drainage material into the base of the container. Until the danger of frost has passed, keep the basket in a frost-free site in good light. Then, when the container is in its growing position, check it daily and water it, taking care not to flush compost and young plants out of the basket.

You can also use pots or wire hanging baskets, with their chains removed, set into pipes or chimney pots. This suits salad leaves, which are going to be cut frequently, so will be in the containers for a relatively short period of time. Plant up more pots in succession, and have them waiting, ready to be brought forward once the original plants have been harvested to exhaustion.

Use plants such as nasturtium, with its sharp-tasting, trailing leaves and flowers, and beet, with colourful salad leaves, to provide colour and contrast to the densely planted salad leaves. Nasturtium flowers are delicious in salads, but remove the green base of the flower, as this is bitter tasting.

In autumn you can have similar collections of salad and stir-fry greens with Oriental leaves, grown from plug plants or home-raised seedlings. This will give you two seasons of excitement in your salad bowl or wok.

Lettuce and salad-leaf seedlings can be closely planted, as you are going to harvest them leaf by leaf, not as whole plants. But tomatoes, peppers, and hearting lettuces need more space and, in the case of tomatoes and peppers would normally be planted one to a pot. They also need deeper containers, so baskets are not suitable for most potted crops. Instead grow them in pots with saucers so they have reservoirs of water during the hot summer months.

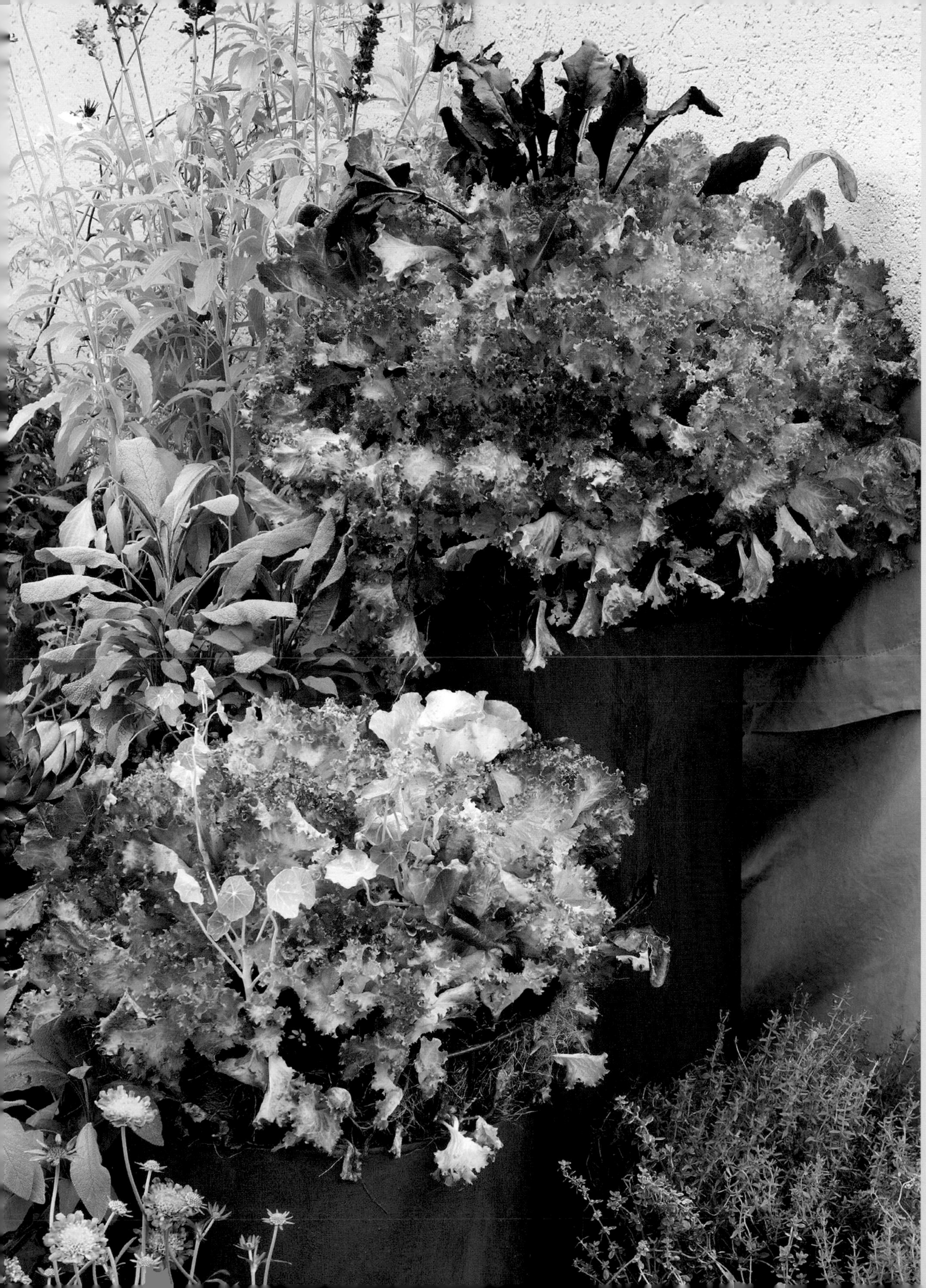

climbing high

plants
- *Clematis florida sieboldii*
- *Fuchsia* 'Celia Smedley'
- *Pelargonium* 'Lord Bute
- *Convolvulus sabatius*

plant alternatives
- Other clematis, such as *C. alpina* or *C. macropetala*
- *Jasminum officinale*
- Sweet peas
- Nasturtiums
- *Ipomea lobata*
- *Ipomea purpurea* 'Star of Yelta'
- *Rhodochiton atrosanguineum*
- *Passiflora*

MATERIALS
- Terracotta containers
- Drainage materials (crocks, polystyrene, gravel)
- Loam-based compost
- Ready-made wigwam support, or willow twigs and string to weave your own
- Wire rings or soft twine

When grouping pots together, it's important to combine plants of different heights. You need tall plants for the back row, medium-height specimens in the middle, and shorter and ground-cover ones towards the front. In the back row you can either use permanent woody plants such as standard trees, permanent climbing plants, or collections of annual climbers, but remember that you will need to provide the climbers with support.

The main height in this collection of pots comes from the climbing plant, a clematis. The fast-growing *Fuchsia* 'Celia Smedley' offers medium height, while the bushy *Pelargonium* 'Lord Bute' provides a compact shape at a lower level. In the foreground, *Convolvulus sabatius* forms a mound of colour.

You can plant container-grown climbers at any time of year; however, early summer planting is suitable, and the support that you provide will give the plant the framework it needs for its spring growth. You can buy a ready-made climbing-plant support or weave your own from flexible twigs of willow or hazel. Plant your climber first, then set your support carefully in position, taking care not to damage your plant's roots. Some climbers will attach and wind themselves through supports, but if you do have to tie in the stems with wire rings or soft twine, take care not to damage young, vulnerable stems. Tie in the stray stems as they grow.

If you have allowed space in the tub for lower-growing plants to establish at the base of the climber, remember that you can change these and swap in new plants as they come into flower. Always take care as you do so that you don't damage or disturb the roots of the clematis unduly.

Clematis florida 'Sieboldii' needs shelter from cold and wind, so grows well nestling among other pots, which offer incidental shelter. In winter, you will need to bring it into a frost-free environment. Trim out dead growth in early spring; hard prune thin, tangled growth, avoiding cutting into the thicker stems, spread out the remaining stems, and tie them separately to their support. Mulch in late spring and apply fertilizer. Keep it well watered.

As an alternative to a permanent or perennial climbing plant, grow annual climbing plants such as sweet peas, morning glory (*Ipomea purpurea*) or the rainbow-coloured *Ipomea lobata*. Tender climbers, such as passion flower and *Rhodochiton atrosanguineum* will need to be taken to a frost-free site in winter.

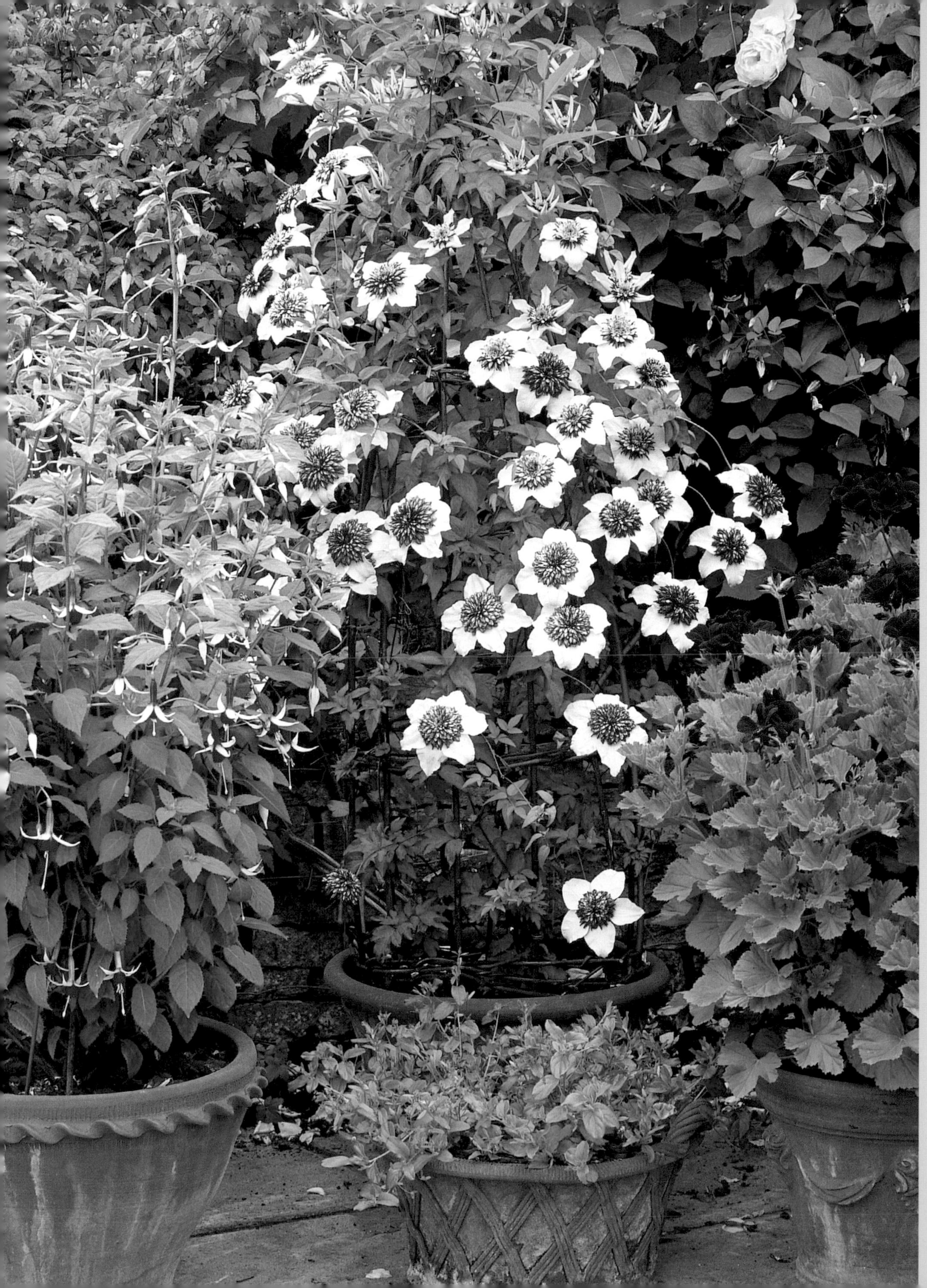

late summer

AT THE HEIGHT OF SUMMER, THERE IS A BRIEF MOMENT WHEN YOU CAN SIT OUTSIDE IN THE SUNSHINE, ENJOYING THE FRAGRANT, FLORAL, AND FOLIAGE BONANZA YOU HAVE CREATED AROUND YOU. ENJOY THE MOMENT — THERE'S MORE TO DO TO KEEP THE CONTAINER GARDEN GROWING.

Herbs are among the best plants for fragrancing your garden, as are roses and lilies. Perfume from plants is at its most intense on still, hot days and evenings, especially if the area is enclosed. Fragrance, more noticeable at night from some species such as the Cape night phlox (*Zaluzianskya capensis*), also comes from exotic tender plants such as brugmansia or angels' trumpets. If you live in a cold area you can bring them out safely into the world in late spring and early summer. In summer they will grow well, so give them plenty of water and an all-purpose fertilizer, and the reward will be a veritable trumpet concerto.

RIGHT
Ornamental grasses, such as *Hakonechloa macra* 'Alboaurea', are a class-act in the garden and even more so in containers. This specimen offers fountain-like mounds of striped citrine-green foliage in spring and summer, flushing a fiery red in autumn.

OPPOSITE
By late summer you can safely enjoy exotic tender plants outdoors such as the fragrant angels' trumpet's (*Brugmansia* 'Jamaica Yellow', the blue-flowered climber plumbago (*Plumbago capensis*), the variegated tropical foliage plant *Sanchezia nobilis*, the succulent *Kalanchoe pumila*, and the palm-leaved *Setaria palmifolia* .

Complete the exotic theme with bananas plants, such as the *Ensete ventricosum* and *Musa* species, which will grow vigorously in summer, offering dramatic foliage, converting the tamest patio into a jungle.

Growing roses in pots

Roses are a particular delight in early summer. Miniature roses, growing to just 45cm (18in) and flowering abundantly through the summer, provide pools of colour that you can slot into place to brighten a foliage-rich corner. Patio roses, are excellent in containers. They are not tall-growing, reaching just 60cm (24in), and are compact in shape, but they are free-flowering, and will make a good show, especially if grown in full sun.

Also good in containers are ground-cover roses, but these do spread, and their long stems will spill over the edge of the container. Patio and ground-cover roses grown in containers need a light cut back in spring. Plant them in pots at least 30cm (12in) deep. Water them well, and top-dress them with a rose fertilizer in spring. Continue foliar feeding regularly and deadhead to keep the flowers coming.

Although they will provide excellent flower colour over a long period, patio and ground-cover roses are not scented. Most types of scented rose will not thrive, nor will they look as good in containers, but you can short-circuit this difficulty by growing scented standard roses, such as a standard 'Margaret Merrill' or 'Mary Rose'. As the central stem is bare, you will need to plant up the area around the rose with frothy and shapely plants, for example lavender or verbena. Standard roses need to be planted with a sturdy stake to give them support and prevent windrock.

Herbs and grasses

Varieties of herbs such as lavender, rosemary, thyme, sage, chamomile, and mint make perfect pot plants. To enjoy their aromas you need to be able to crush or brush past the foliage to release aromatic oils. Rosemary and lavender can be topiarized into interesting forms, or left to grow into their natural shape.

OPPOSITE
Fuchsias are among the stars of the container scene. They come in so many colour combinations, and provide brilliance over a long period in summer, but they need winter protection. *Fuchsia* 'Thalia' also has attractive foliage.

ABOVE
Miniature roses, such as *Rosa* 'Queen Mother', can be used for spot colour on their own, or as an instant burst in a larger container. For a bushier effect, grow a patio rose, such as *Rosa* 'Sweet Dream', which makes a taller plant, is scented, and is reliably floriferous through the summer.

Thyme comes in upright shrubby forms, as well as prostrate, low-growing plants, making it suitable for the edges of pots, from where it can trail, as well as a central position. These herbs are all drought-tolerant and will grow well in full sun. Pots are just right to contain mint, which always over-exceeds its allotted space in any garden in no time at all.

Even a chamomile lawn, a one-time traditional feature of large gardens, is not beyond the dreams of the container gardener. Buy six plants of *Chamaemelum nobile* 'Treneague', and plant them up in an attractive terracotta pot, in a loam-based compost with added grit. Keep it close at hand on the patio and let your fingers, instead of feet, do the walking to release its heavenly pineapple fragrance and lift your spirits at the end of a day.

Grasses – not lawn ones, but ornamental grasses, and grass-like plants – are among the most versatile plants you can use in containers. Some are upright-growing, producing unbending flower stems among their foliage in summer and autumn; some are fountain-like and produce their flowers on wispy stems; and others beg for their shocks of wig-like foliage to be combed and groomed.

Whichever ornamental grasses you choose, they will add inestimably to the style of your plantings. They also offer variety in terms of foliage colour – some are variegated, while some offer grey-blue, bronze, sandy, and even purple foliage. Their seedheads develop in late summer on arching stems that bend in the breeze, offering the dimension of movement to otherwise static plant collections.

The flowers and foliage, even when past their best at the end of autumn, are worth leaving in place until spring. During winter, should there be a frost, grasses take on this cold element, frosting into sherbet-like cocktails stirrers and straws.

In spring, when the new foliage of ornamental grasses begins to shoot through, you can comb and tease out the old foliage and flower stems. Wear gloves to protect against cutting or spiking your hands.

Heat and colour

In terms of colour, it is always possible to turn the heat up by several degrees. Combine plants such as cannas, dahlias, sunflowers, gazanias, osteospermums, and arctotis to set the container garden on fire with the glowing warmth of their red, orange, and yellow flowers. Cannas also have fiery tones in their foliage. If the tone needs cooling down, use the cool, citrine-green, blue or silvery foliage of plants such as hostas and feathery ferns, as well as white-flowered plants, including the pinky-white *Gaura lindheimeri* and white forms of dianthus.

Fuchsias are versatile container plants that come in a range of heights and shapes. You can find bushy, trailing, or upright fuchsias, the latter lending themselves to training as standards, which will offer height to a container collection.

Bulbous plants for summer pots include lilies, gladiolus, tuberous begonias, dahlias, and agapanthus. Planted in spring, they need regular watering and feeding to encourage them to thrust their stems upwards.

Dahlias and pots are a natural combination, as most gardeners lift

OPPOSITE
Terracotta and agaves are natural partners, the earthy look of the pot making a perfect foil for the spiky plant. But this pot will prove difficult when you come to repot the agave; it will be tricky to remove the plant without damaging the pot. If you can, use a pot like this more as a cache pot than a permanent container, or leave it unplanted to make its own architectural statement.

ABOVE
An example of living dangerously. Plants that go with the flow and wave in the wind, such as ornamental grasses and phormiums, will survive in roof-garden sites. Water them well as wind will dry out the compost and can stress plant foliage.

RIGHT
Plants that need different composts, such as these azaleas and osteospermums, can be used in combination, provided that you keep them in their individual pots and use the designer container as a cache pot.

To be at their best in summer, some plants like it hot with a dash of shade; lilies, for example, prefer a cool root run. Others, such as agapanthus, enjoy baking in full sun, and want the whole pot to themselves. Mexican grass plants thrive in the hottest position in summer, but need to winter indoors in cool climes.

Clockwise from above: *Agapanthus* 'Albus'; *Dasylirion longissimum*, above a sea of New Zealand *Acaena caesiiglauca*; *Lilium* 'Golden Joy' with *Thymus* 'Bertram Anderson' at its feet.

them out of the garden and keep them dormant over the winter in a frost-free site. If you keep them in containers, you can more easily lift them from their flowering site in the garden or their positions on the patio into shelter in winter. Some gardeners avoid dahlias, finding them too garish and vulgar, but in the container context they are versatile. Their colour range, flower shapes, and, in many cases, deep bronze-to- purple foliage win them a star role.

Combine dahlias with cannas – tropical plants that are becoming highly popular – for double the foliage and flower effect. Cannas have large oval leaves that can be heavily marked with pink, orange, and bronze stripes, depending on the variety. The flowers take their time to appear, providing brightly coloured, bird-like blooms, and ornamental seedcases in late summer and early autumn.

Like dahlias, cannas need to be lifted and stored over the winter in a dormant state in frost-free conditions, so containers suit them well. You can place both cannas and dahlias as specimens into the border in their pots, removing them to shelter when they have done their dash, and the first frosts have withered their foliage. Alternatively, grow them in mixed containers on the patio, enjoying them for their stunning foliage and flowers before moving them into storage.

Agapanthus need to be crowded and pot-bound in the container to flower well. If they become too large for the container, move them into a pot that is only slightly bigger.

Lilies should be at their best at this time of year, offering you fragrant and colourful flowers that will dramatically turn up the heat in colour terms, as they are available in hot oranges and bright yellows, as well as in deepest midnight purple, while cool white lilies will add elegance to a dark-foliage shrub border. Keep them well watered and remove spent flowerheads as they fade, taking care not to get the pollen on your clothes.

Architectural forms

Succulents and cacti thrive in the late summer sunshine. These spiky plants, whether they are large and chunky agaves, or small and geometric in shape, such as echevarias, have tons of architectural attitude, which makes an attractive foil to some of the fluffier floral delights of the season. Team them in single plantings with other individual pots of silvery foliage plants, white-flowered marguerites and shimmering pink ivy-leaf pelargoniums. Larger specimens such as agave, always work well in combinations, but they don't need to be partnered, standing alone with great majesty.

Because their leaves and stems are adapted to store water, they are a gift to slothful container gardeners,

Right
Turn up the heat by grouping hot-coloured flowering plants with sun-loving palms. Here, the purple foliage of *Cordyline australis* and the green fan-like leaves of the palm (*Chaemerops humilis*) are set on fire with the orange tones of *Streptosolen jamesonii* and helianthemum, combined with the fire-engine red of verbena and *Monarda* 'Cambridge Scarlet'. At the centre of the collection, cooling it down by a degree or two, is the variegated ornamental grass, *Acorus gramineus* 'Ogon'.

as they really do thrive in sun and well-drained soil, needing water as and when their compost feels dry. If the weather is wet, make sure that the plants are not sitting in saucers of rainwater.

From your vegetable pots you will be harvesting lettuces and salad leaves, as well as radishes and new potatoes. Cordon tomatoes need to be tied in to the supporting stakes, and all the vegetable pots will need to be watered regularly.

Looking ahead

Now is the time to put autumn-flowering bulbs, such as colchicums, autumn-flowering cyclamen, and the yellow *Sternbergia lutea* into pots. Use a loam-based compost with added grit, and plant them in deep containers. Although colchicums are the real harbingers of autumn, they offer lovely mauve or white crocus-like flowers that push through the compost and provide colour throughout the season. In spring, they send up a mass of large lanky leaves. At this stage move the pot out of sight, but allow the leaves to die down naturally, feeding with bulb fertilizer, just as you did when you fed your spring-flowering bulbs after their flowering period had finished.

Towards the end of summer, bulbs will start to appear in garden centres and at nurseries, or you can order them from specialist mail-order bulb catalogues. Buy fresh healthy ones and plant them as soon as you can.

Keep on deadheading all the flowers in your pots as they die, and always keep the surface of containers weed-free, as the weeds compete with your container plants for food and moisture.

OPPOSITE
A climbing plant in a container, such as *Clematis* 'Alionushka' is useful as a device to provide height in an area of the garden holding relatively low-growing plants. Here, it rises above a quartet of closely clipped box balls in a parterre garden.

ABOVE
Looking for all the world as if they had stepped out of a cowboy-style cinema set, these succulent candelabra-shaped euphorbia need to be taken into frost-free shelter in winter.

RIGHT
Cabbage 'January King' and neighbouring tomatoes are ready for harvest. Renew the compost once you have removed all the cabbages, before replanting with another vegetable crop.

lightning strikes

Even in areas where there is no soil for planting direct into the ground, you can introduce light and colour by using brilliant combinations of foliage and flowering plants in several containers of different sizes as short-term bolts of lightning. Some of them can be left in place for a reasonable length of time, while pots of flowering plants can be replaced as their blooms fade.

In the background, permanent plantings in the ground of ivy and *Fatsia japonica*, with their variegated and shiny evergreen foliage offer a degree of brightness to the area, but an injection of colour, in the shape of container plantings will provide the extra "oomph" necessary to increase the visual interest where it is difficult to grow plants directly in the ground.

Plants such as carex, with its thin, strappy, always tousled foliage, offers a torch-like glow, complementing nicely the dainty yellow flowers of *Sanvitalia procumbens*, a low-growing perennial that is usually treated as an annual. *Sanvitalia* grows best in full sun, so place it in the foreground, where it will benefit from the brightest situation. If its flowers start to flag, replace it with a fresh plant, or a different variety that offers the same effect, such as *Bidens ferulifolia* or *Bacopa* 'Baja'. Carex grows well in shade or sun, but needs careful watering in a container.

At the heart of the grouping, lantana, abutilon, and the ornamental grass or purple millet, *Pennisetum glaucum*, provide a flame-like shaft of colour at various levels in the container. Lantana is a half-hardy perennial. It won't survive outdoor frosts, so unless you have a place where it can overwinter, treat it as a summer bedding plant. It thrives in sun and needs good drainage, but provides a rich show of flowers in a range of orange, cream, and yellow. It combines well with the apricot and yellow tones of hybrid forms of the flowering maple, *Abutilon* x *hybridum*. Abutilon flowers continuously through the summer, but it needs to be overwintered in a frost-free site, if you want to keep it from year to year. As they are all planted in the same container, it will be possible to take them into a frost-free shelter, if you have the space. Keep them on the dry side during the winter, and top-dress and begin to feed and water them as the weather warms in late spring.

Ornamental grasses are popular for containers, and the purple foliage of the *Pennisetum glaucum* is one of the best foils for flowering plants and for giving height. It is best treated as a half-hardy annual and replaced annually. In spring its foliage is light green, darkening to a rich burgundy purple.

plants
- *Sanvitalia procumbens*
- *Carex comans* 'Bronze'
- *Lantana camara* hybrids
- *Abutilon* x *hybridum*
- *Pennisetum glaucum* 'Purple Majesty'

plant alternatives
- *Bidens ferulifolia*
- *Bacopa* 'Baja'
- Ornamental grasses
- Hostas
- Dahlias
- Osteospermums

MATERIALS
- Containers of various shapes and sizes
- Drainage material (crocks, polystyrene, gravel)
- Loam-based compost
- Added grit

pretty and pink

plants
- *Verbena rigida*
- *Argyranthemum* cultivars
- *Salvia officinalis* 'Purpurascens'
- *Verbena* x *hybrida*

plant alternatives
- *Argyranthemum* 'Jamaica Primrose'
- *Tropaeoleum majus* 'Moonlight' (nasturtium)
- *Oenothera macrocarpa*
- Golden thyme
- Golden sage (*Salvia officinalis* 'Icterina')

MATERIALS
- Ceramic container
- Drainage materials (crocks, polystyrene, gravel)
- Loam-based compost
- Added grit

There are many wonderful colour combinations to try in container plantings, and they can be achieved by clever mixing of flowers and foliage. They will provide colour throughout the summer.

If your ceramic containers do not have drainage holes, you can make them by drilling into the base of the pot. This is a delicate operation, and you will need a steady hand. Place a strip of masking tape across the base of the pot and use an electric drill with a small masonry bit to make a number of small holes.

Once you have filled the drainage layer into the pot and added some compost in a loose layer, work from the centre of the pot adding the various plants. Place the marguerite (*Argyranthemum*) in the middle. Its silvery foliage is an attractive foil to the pink flowers and will tone well with the mauve foliage of the sage. Several pink forms are available, including those with double and single flowers. At the back of the planting there is another verbena, *Verbena rigida*, which grows to 45cm (18in) and has long thin flower stems with branched flowerheads. Half-hardy, these plants need winter protection.

For long-lasting mauve-pink foliage choose the purple sage (*Salvia officinalis* 'Purpurascens'). It will produce flower stems in summer with blue flowers. You can either let it flower or cut the flowering stems back to encourage a bushier, more compact growth. You could also use the tri-coloured sage (*Salvia officinalis* 'Tricolor'), which has soft pink-mauve, green, and white in its leaves.

Finally, place the low-growing trailing hybrid verbenas around the edge of the pot. Cut them back if they get too straggly later in the growing season to encourage flowering. To keep the flowering going until the first frosts, cut off or pinch out the spent flowers on a regular basis. Then you can either pot up the half-hardy plants and bring them into shelter or move the whole pot into shelter. You can remove and repot the sage, saving it for next year. It will grow well through the winter outdoors in cool temperate climates.

As an alternative to the many marguerite and verbena hyrids available, try the buttery yellow of *A*. 'Jamaica Primrose' and combine it with the golden foliage of a citrine-green thyme or with the golden sage (*Salvia officinalis* 'Icterina'), and the lemony flowers of Nasturtium 'Moonlight'. For evening colour and fragrance use the evening primrose (*Oenothera macrocarpa*). At the end of the season you would need to protect 'Jamaica Primrose'. The nasturtium may survive a mild winter, but as it is best grown as an annual, you should remove it from the planting when you lift the argyranthemum.

a jungle theme

Large leaves combined with exotic-looking flowers fit the image most of us have of a tropical jungle, and in gardens this is a popular theme. In pots the same bold effect can be created, with a wide range of luxuriant foliage and jazzy flowering plants.

By combining hardy and tender plants selected for their exotic foliage and flowers you can bring the jungle in a container to your patio or a particularly warm sheltered site in the garden.

Tall plants, including *Ensete ventricosum, Aralia elata,* and *Hedychium aurantiacum,* with lush, large, or small foliage and grasses, such as miscanthus, provide the backbone of the collection. They need to be in large individual pots or planted direct into a large "hold-all" container.

Once you have the foliage and tall plants in place, add lower-growing, bushy plants, such as the purple- or dark-leaved dahlias, *Heuchera* 'Palace Purple', shorter grasses, such as *Elymus magellanicus,* and hostas.

The flower colour in the selection comes from trailing or tall-stemmed annuals and perennials that weave through the foliage framework.

Dark-leaved dahlias are doubly useful, as their dark foliage adds mystery and depth to the group, and their flowers are usually bright and exotic-looking. Hostas also provide this double attraction with green, golden, or grey foliage, and spikes of tubular flowers. *Hedychium auriantiacum* is a ginger lily, with very shapely and distinctive flowers and foliage.

Annuals, including the spider flower, *Cleome hassleriana,* in white or mauve, and *Spilanthes oleracea* 'Peek-a-boo', a summer bedding favourite, with bobble-like yellow and red flowers, provide spots of colour at different heights within the display. Tender perennials, such as the arum lily, provide extra flower and foliage power. The arum lily, *Zantedeschia aethiopica,* is white-flowered, but there are many cultivars with yellow, mauve, and dark purple flowers, that can be used for quick colour effects.

The tender and half-hardy plants such as ensete, bananas, hedychiums, cannas, melianthus, scadoxus, solenostemon, zantedeschia, dahlia, and aralia, need to be taken out of the main collection and overwintered in a frost-free situation. Then, next year, they can be brought back into the jungle scene when all danger of frost has passed.

plants

- *Ensete ventricosum*
- *Hedychium aurantiacum*
- *Melianthus major*
- *Heuchera* 'Palace Purple'
- *Cleome hassleriana*
- *Miscanthus* species
- *Zantedeschia* cultivars
- *Spilanthes oleracea*
- *Aralia elata*
- *Elymus magellanicus*

plant alternatives

- *Scadoxus multiflorus* ssp. *katherinae*
- *Miscanthus sinensis* 'Kleine Silberspinne'
- *Miscanthus sinensis* 'Zebrinus'
- *Dahlia* 'Bishop of Llandaff'
- *Dahlia* 'Arabian Night'
- *Pennisetum glaucum* 'Purple Majesty'
- *Hosta* 'Halcyon'
- *Canna indica*
- *Solenostemon* (coleus)

MATERIALS

- Copper container, and individual pots
- Drainage material (crocks, gravel)
- Charcoal (to keep compost sweet, if pot has no drainage hole)
- Loam-based compost with added grit

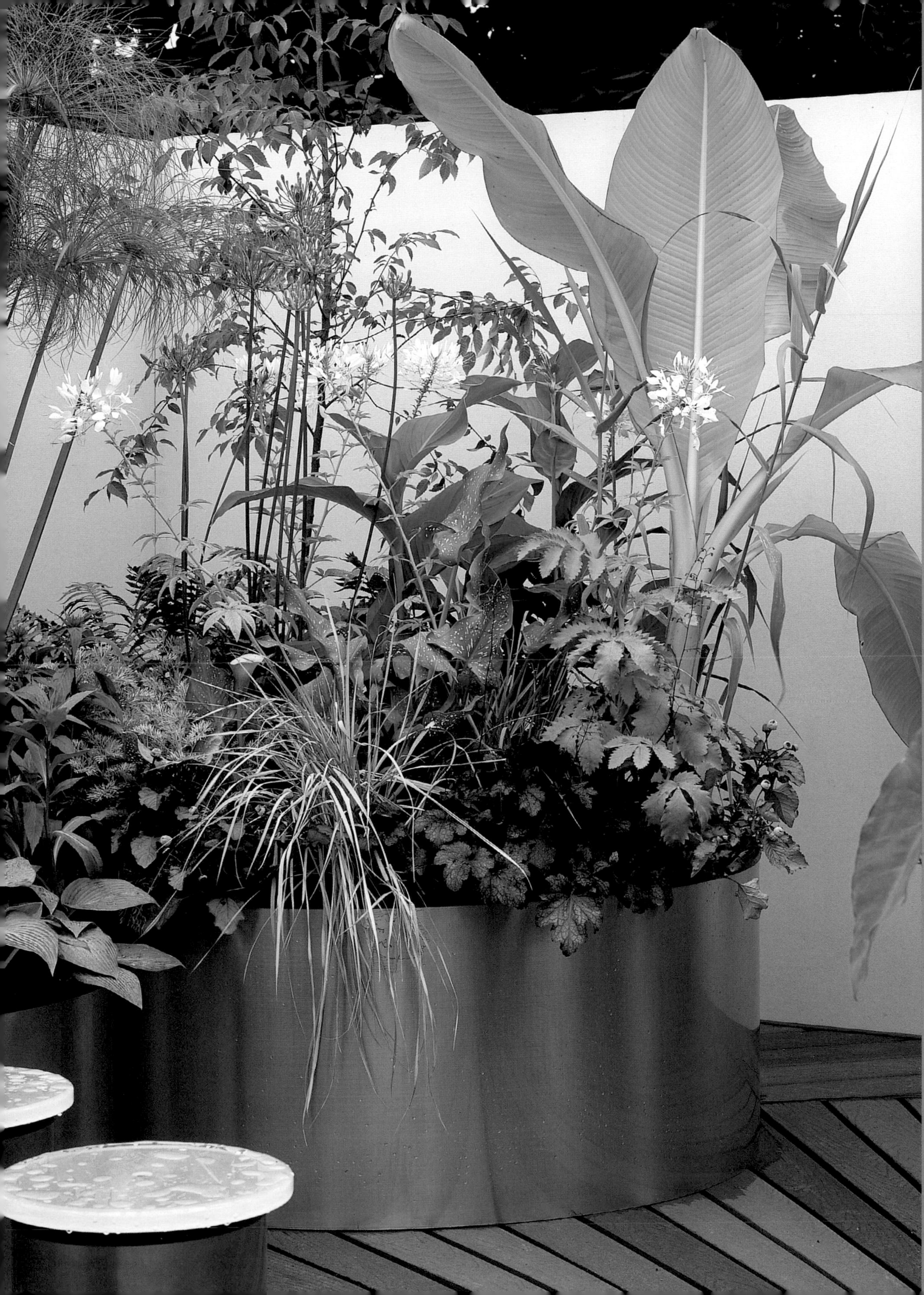

autumn

PERENNIAL SHRUBS AND EVERGREEN
TREES GROWN SOLO IN CONTAINERS
COME INTO THEIR OWN AT THIS TIME
OF YEAR, AS THEIR FOLIAGE WILL BE
THE MAINSTAY OF THE SEASON.
ARCHITECTURAL PLANTS WITH STRONG
FOLIAGE WILL STAND OUT PARTICULARLY
WELL, AS WILL GRASSES.

Although evergreen plants will
continue to provide greens, golds,
and variegated foliage, autumn
heralds a farewell to the wider
varieties of colour and form present
in summer. Even so, there is still
much to do in the container garden
to tidy it up for the winter, and to
prepare for the springtime return of
a full spectrum of colour.

Cutting back, moving on

Despite the fact that the natural
growth rate of plants is slowing
down in autumn, it is still a busy time
of year for you, with planting and
thinking ahead for spring, cutting
back, and harvesting fruit and
vegetables from your container crop
pots. Cutting back spent flowerheads
will keep blooms going for as long as
possible, and may result in a flush of
new leaves just before autumn ends.

Lavender gets a bit of a short back
and sides in summer when you pick
its flowers for creating fragrance
sachets. Now is the time to cut back
the stems of herbs such as lavender
and sage to about one third of their
length. If you have a large quantity,
keep some of the stems in a dry place
and save them to create aromatic

fires in winter. This is also the last
time of year to cut back box plants,
and to trim them into formal or
whimsical topiary shapes.

Autumn is the traditional time to
lift and divide clumps of perennial
plants that have grown too big for
their pots. This increases your supply
of pot subjects, and ensures that the
plants are not congested.

It is also a time to cosset plants,
so I bring tender lavenders, and
other vunerable perennials, such as
standard lemon verbena plants,
which would normally be hardy, into
the greenhouse or conservatory to
overwinter in safety.

Take the opportunity to see what
is looking good at the local garden
centre, and think how you could

ABOVE
In autumn your container plants work hard
to delight. The bromeliad *Fascicularia bicolor*
is one such plant that provides a blazing
catherine wheel of colour as its inner leaves
mature to a fiery red.

OPPOSITE
Dahlia 'Fascination' and *D.* 'Piper's Pink' will
keep on flowering into autumn, as long as
their foliage is not hit by frosts. Once this
happens, take the dahlias into frost-free
shelter for the winter. *Paulownia tomentosa*,
grown here for its splendid deciduous
foliage, may also need protection, so that its
roots don't freeze.

Herbs can play a double role in your potted collection – use them to spice up your cooking, and, if evergreen, they'll provide interest and colour all year round. Growing herbs in pots means that you can have a herb garden that's handy for the kitchen, out on the back patio or by the front door, instead of having to wade over a soggy lawn or down a muddy path to pick them.

Clockwise from top: thyme (*Thymus* 'Bertram Anderson'); bay (*Laurus nobilis*); and Tri-coloured sage (*Salvia officinalis* 'Tricolor').

ABOVE
Ornamental grasses, such as *Stipa tenuissima*, continue to be graceful in autumn, although some may look as if they need a good session at the hairdressers.

LEFT
Succulents, such as echevaria, will have a last fling in the autumn container garden. Don't leave them outside if frost is forecast.

OPPOSITE
Japanese maples, such as *Acer palmatum* f. *atropurpureum* and *A.p.* 'Ozakazuki' come into their own in autumn as their foliage colours up before it falls.

weave some seasonal flowering plants, such as chrysanthemums, into your planting schemes.

The hot colours that predominate in summer continue in autumn, in some cases fleetingly, as the foliage of some trees and shrubs in containers take on their brilliant autumn tones before falling. The rewards of evergreen trees and shrubs are longer term, but deciduous plants that lose their foliage provide such a fiery crackle of colour as they depart that I think they are worth the effort. Japanese maples and *Berberis thunbergii* are among the plants that deserve a place in the autumn container garden for this reason.

You are likely to see bundles of wallflowers on offer in garden centres at this time. Plant them up in autumn, and they will produce a colourful display in late spring and early summer.

Containers need to work harder in autumn to provide interest, so look for unusual plants to achieve stylish effects. One such choice that holds centre stage in autumn is the bromeliad, *Fascicularia bicolor*. Its strappy outer leaves remain green, while the inner rosette colours up like a blazing catherine wheel in autumn. It is frost-tender, so needs winter protection in cool climates. It does best in very well-drained compost with added grit, and needs only moderate water in summer, and extremely little in winter.

Dahlias and cannas will continue to give their all in terms of flowers and foliage until they are damaged by the first frosts. When this happens, cut back the stems and foliage, lift the tubers out of their pots and store them in boxes of peat, where they can be kept dry and frost-free during their dormant winter period. Alternatively, you can leave them in their pots, but you will still need to keep them in dry and frost-free shelter. However you store them, take care not to damage the tubers, as they may rot.

Autumn is a good time to assess the success of your spring and summer planting schemes. Some may have worked better than others, so you might wish to repeat the good ones and write off the combinations or plants that didn't perform well. This is also the right moment to look through the gardening catalogues and choose the plants and colour combinations that will brighten the following year in your container garden.

Starting afresh

Even though autumn may feel like it is all about removals and cutbacks, this is also a time to start again. Bulbs hold so much promise for spring – planting up containers of shapely bulbs seems almost like an act of faith. Luckily, they do come up, and provide the container gardener with an array of colour in spring. By choosing bulbs carefully, you can have pots of colour from late winter through to late spring. Snowdrops and *Iris reticulata* will kick the flowering season off again in midwinter, with crocusses, narcissus, and tulips following in stages through the spring.

There are so many bulbs to choose from, but using a single type per container results in a better overall look to the planting, and you can be sure that they will all flower

together. This also means that once the flowering period is over you can simply remove the bulb pots from the container site and allow them to die down out of sight.

You can plant bulbs in tiers so you can pack more into the containers. They will all flower at roughly the same time, and provide a full and flower-packed punch. Alternatively, you may decide to plant bulbs with different flowering times in tiers, to give you a longer flowering period.

I prefer to grow bulbs of single varieties or species in small pots that I drop into spaces in larger containers, just as the bulbs are beginning to flower. Then, when they have finished flowering, I remove them, pot and all, from the main containers and replace them with pots of new bulbs or other flowering plants as the season advances. If you don't have the space to grow your own plant inserts, you will find that garden centres are filled with a wonderful choice of bulbs in pots that can be used in this way for instant and short-term effects.

LEFT
Flower colour in autumn comes in a range of short-term plants, such as chrysanthemums, often known as 'Florist's Mums' and usually used as indoor plants over winter. You can use them, together with pom-pom dahlias, the coloured foliage plant *Solenostemon* (coleus), and *Fuchsia* 'Thalia', until the first frosts cut them back. Overwinter fuchsia and coleus in frost-free shelter if you can.

OPPOSITE
Keep the colours of autumn going with a collection of pots holding grasses such as *Carex* 'Evergold' and shrubs including *Berberis thunbergii* 'Red Pillar'. Once the berberis loses its leaves, move it off-stage and replace it with an evergreen to take you through the winter.

instant autumn colour

plants
- *Cotoneaster frigidus* 'Cornubia'
- *Gaultheria procumbens*
- *Skimmia japonica* ssp. *reevesiana*
- Cyclamen hybrids

plant alternatives
- Japanese maples
- Chrysanthemums (sold widely in flower, in pots)
- *Pernettya mucronata*
- Heathers
- *Cyclamen hederifolium*

MATERIALS
- Terracotta pot
- Ericaceous compost
- Drainage material (crocks, polystyrene, gravel)
- Hazelnut-shell mulch

Many garden centres will group together the best plants for autumn foliage, berries, and flower colour. You can then pick and mix to make your own seasonal planting that will give you maximum colour and interest from autumn through into winter.

You can achieve these quick seasonal container transformations easily, but some of the plants shown here have special needs and should be potted up into larger containers as they mature. *Cotoneaster* 'Cornubia' is one such plant. In the ground it will grow to 6m (19ft), with a similar spread. A container will restrict its growth, but you will need to pot it on from year to year into larger vessels. Of course, if you have a garden you could consider planting it out after it has done its instant autumn dash in the container. It is fully hardy and needs good drainage to thrive. It produces abundant clusters of red fruits and arching, semi-evergreen branches.

Gaultheria procumbens, an acid-loving, low-growing, ground-covering, perennial, shrubby plant, needs an ericaceous compost. Its small oval leaves turn purple-bronze in autumn and winter, and it produces deep-red berries in autumn. The other plants in the collection don't need the lime-free compost, but will tolerate the ericaceous conditions.

The other berried plant in the collection is a skimmia: *Skimmia japonica* ssp. *reevesiana*. This is a low-growing shrub with aromatic foliage and small white flowers in spring, followed in autumn by deep red berries.

If all three of the red-berried plants are fired up with their clusters of fruit, a deep-red cyclamen with mottled grey-green foliage will add the perfect finishing touch to this instant autumn collection. Keep the cyclamen in its pot and bring it into shelter when frosts are forecast. Don't worry unduly if you lose the cyclamens – hybrids of this flower are so inexpensive and widely available that you can replace them with another one already in bloom for a short period.

Alternatively, you can use the species cyclamen, *Cyclamen hederifolium*, which has flowers in autumn, then produces wonderfully marbled foliage, which will look good over a long period after flowering is over.

The surface of the compost can be covered with a mulch to help it retain moisture. Here, hazelnut shells have been used to make an unusual and decorative mulch.

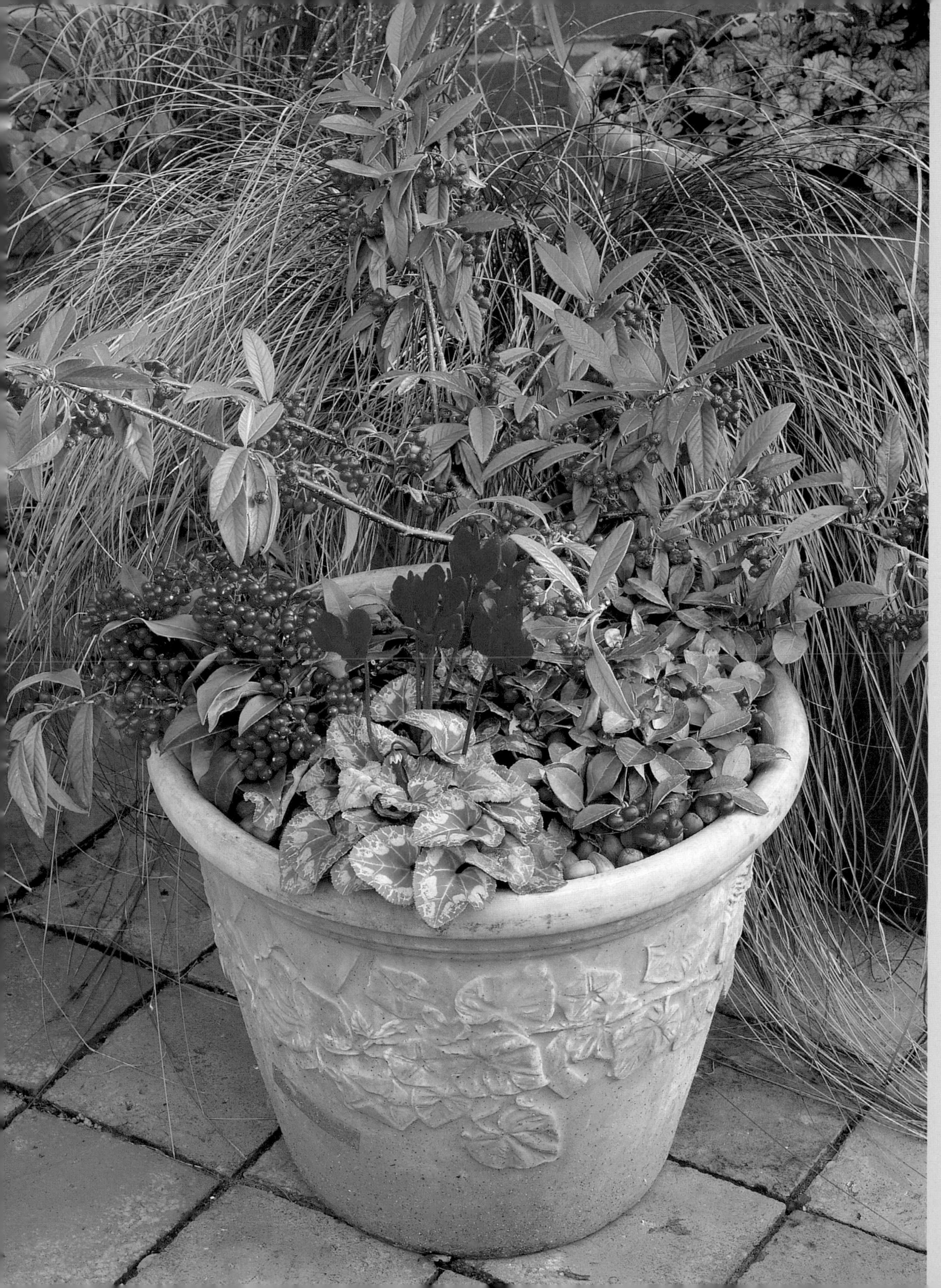

pots of spring colour

plants
- Tulips
- Hyacinths
- Daffodils
- Grape hyacinths
- Amaryllis or hippeastrum

plant alternatives
- Crocus
- Snowdrops
- *Allium karavatiense*
- *Anemone blanda*
- *Anemone coronaria*
- *Fritillaria meleagris*
- *Fritallaria pyrenaica*
- *Fritillaria imperialis* (Crown imperials)
- *Iris reticulata*

MATERIALS
- As many pots of various sizes as you need
- Soil-less compost/bulb fibre
- Loam-based compost with added grit for fritillaries, crocuses, and snowdrops
- Drainage material (crocking, polystyrene, gravel)

Pots and bulbs were made for each other. Planting bulbs in autumn to provide the brightest and most welcome spring colour is one of the great joys of container gardening.

You can plant up a complete spring design using bulbs and evergreens such as ivy, skimmia, and heathers. The evergreens will provide your scheme with some colour and shape through the winter, with the bulbs coming through in spring. But remember that ageing, messy, bulb foliage, although important in producing energy for the bulb to store for next year's growth, is not very attractive once the bulb has finished flowering.

To avoid this, I would suggest growing individual pots of bulbs in separate groupings of named varieties. This way you get strong blocks of colour that are likely to flower at the same time. When they have finished flowering, you can move the pots "off-stage" and leave them to die down in the pots. At this point you need to provide a good foliar feed. You can also heel them into an area in the garden for the same purpose, but don't forget to feed them.

All bulbs need good drainage, so add a good layer of crocks to the base of the pot. Use a fresh, soil-less compost or special "bulb" compost. Some bulbs, such as fritillaries, crocuses, and snowdrops, will need added grit in the compost for extra drainage. Fill the pot with compost to the required depth. Tulips and hyacinths must be planted to a depth of 15cm (6in); narcissus to a depth of 12.5cm (5in).

You can plant them in layers and quite crowded in the pot to ensure a really stunning display at flowering time. Once the bulbs are in place, fill the pot with compost and firm it in gently. Don't let the compost dry out, so water it regularly. If you have crowded the plants in layers in the pots, it will be necessary to repot them after flowering, so that they have space in which to recover and build up the reserves they need for flowering next year. Feed them at this stage.

The hippeastrum or amaryllis is the only exception to the above, as they are bulbs for indoor flowering. They may have been specially prepared so that they are in bloom indoors early in winter, with some in flower before Christmas. A number are specially pre-treated so that they can be given as gifts for the festive season, and will flower later. Plant them so that at least one third of the bulb is above soil level, in a pot that fits the bulb snugly. Once the bulb starts growing, feed it regularly with a high-potash liquid feed, but water it sparingly until the flower bud appears.

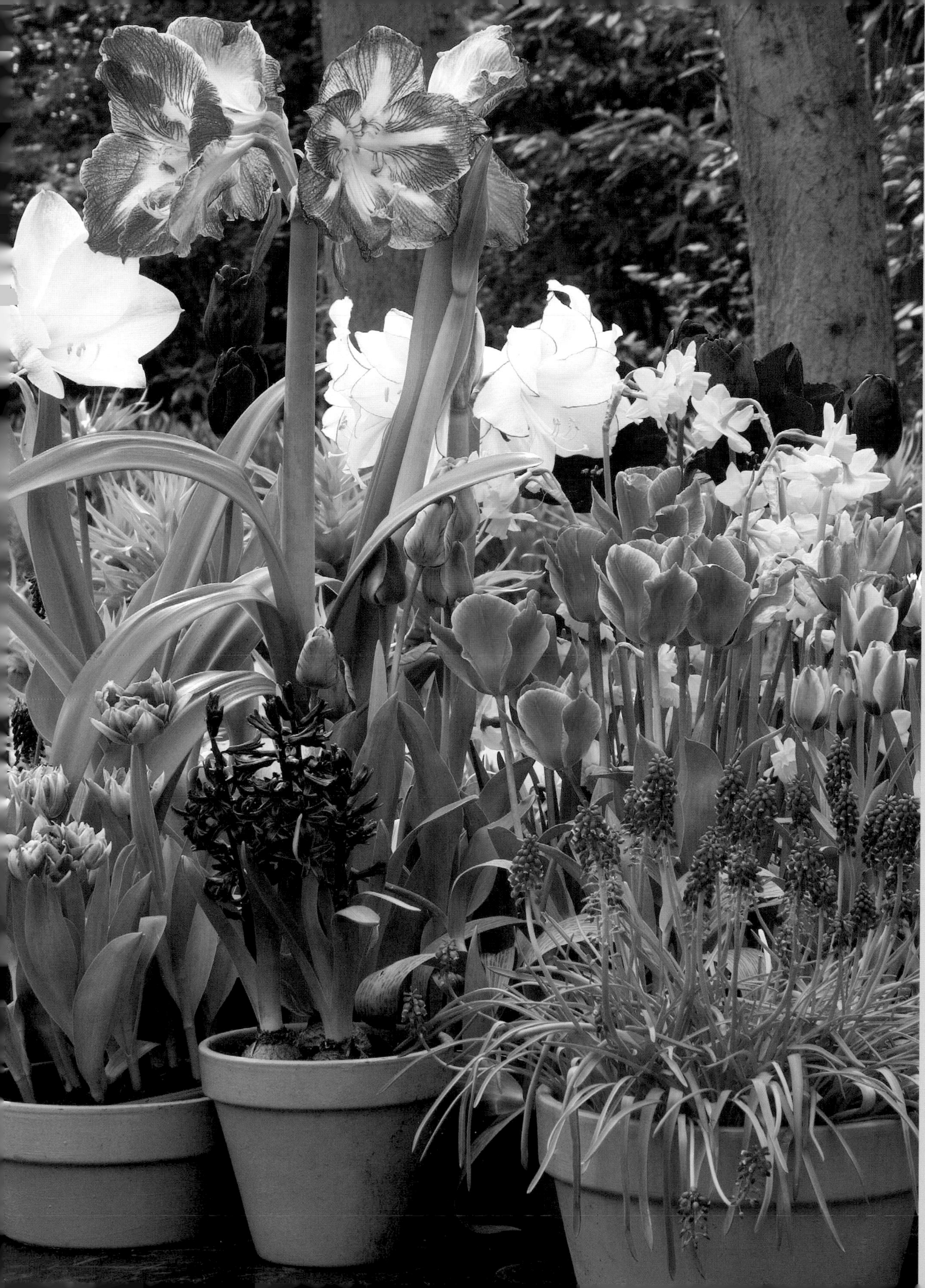

winter

DON'T THINK THAT, JUST BECAUSE IT IS WINTER, YOU WILL HAVE NOTHING TO DO IN YOUR GARDEN, NOR THAT THERE WILL BE VERY LITTLE GROWING TO BRIGHTEN YOUR DAY. ON THE CONTRARY, YOU WILL FIND THAT YOU ARE KEPT BUSY WITH VARIOUS MAINTENANCE TASKS, AS WELL AS PLANNING NEXT YEAR'S SHOWSTOPPERS. AND YOU WILL SOON DISCOVER WHICH PLANTS GIVE YOU ORNAMENT, INSTANT AND SHORT-TERM, AS WELL AS THOSE THAT PROVIDE INTEREST FOR THE LONG HAUL THROUGH WINTER.

Now that the reign of bright summer-bedding and autumnal colour is past, it is possible to assess the bare bones, the skeleton of your container garden. In winter, although the overwhelming choice of summer isn't available, there is still scope for successful, but opportunist, and, probably short-term plants that can be drafted in to plug the gaps left by the previous season's stars.

Evergreen trees and shrubs, such as holly, box, yew, skimmia, pieris, and euonymus, will be among the plants that will fill the seasonal spaces and truly shine at this time.

Even though these plants will not be growing at the same rate as they would in spring and summer, they still need water, so check their compost and don't let it dry out. But, at the same time, remember that drainage is still important. Make sure that the plant roots are not waterlogged. Remove any plant saucers, so that containers are not resting in water.

Colour, texture, and form

Even in winter, in the small space of a container, it is possible to create a variety of styles. A reduced palette of one colour with foliage plants will provide a vibrant formality. Foliage plants with leaves in shades of silver and grey are popular together in containers. Use plain and variegated ivy and box, as well as hardy ferns. Ivy is particularly useful if grown on shaped wire to give a topiary effect.

For colour try the Laser series of cyclamen, which will flower in autumn but may need frost protection. Primulas and winter-flowering pansies are also among the pleasures of winter gardening.

ABOVE
A trio of blue-glazed ceramic pots is filled with plants that will bridge the hungry gap between autumn and spring. They hold *Carex* 'Evergold', *Acorus gramineus* 'Ogon', and the berried *Skimmia japonica* ssp. *reevesiana*.

OPPOSITE
Empty pots can hold just as much promise as full ones. This terracotta urn, with its sculpted lizard, is no exception, rising as it does out of a sea of winter-flowering and ground-covering ericas.

Plants with interesting coloured stems, such as dogwoods and willows, will help to create visual interest. These deciduous shrubs offer bare, red, yellow-green, and ochre stems that provide thin, defined, high points to container designs.

Twisted stems of corkscrew hazel and contorted willow are also useful for creating delicate woodland themes for your winter containers. Witchhazel, with its frazzled yellow and orange flowers on bare stems, is an alternative choice.

Ivy is particularly useful for covering the surface of pots, giving a light and lacy look to the overall planting. There are so many wonderful ivies to choose from: varieties with small, arrow-like foliage; those with buttery-yellow leaves, and myriads of variegated forms. Bugle (*Ajuga reptans*), with its purple-bronze foliage, is another of my favourite plants for covering the surface of a winter container.

LEFT
Even in the depths of winter and in the small space of a container it is possible to create a variety of styles. Use plants with interestingly coloured stems, such as dogwood (*Cornus cericea* 'Flaviramea') for a delicate linear effect among a low-growing collection of winter-flowering pansies and *Euonymus japonicus* 'Microphyllus Pulchellus'.

OPPOSITE
Using mainly evergreen shrubs and ivy, you can create a woodland look. *Cornus alba* 'Westonbirt' and contorted hazel (*Corylus avellana* 'Contorta') form the backdrop, with heuchera, ivy, *Gaultheria procumbens*, and the blue fir (*Picea purgens* 'Blaukissen') at ground level. At the centre of the planting is a double-flowered white primrose and a carex. These will continue to make a good display through the winter, but in time you may wish to remove the dogwood, hazel, and fir, as they will need more space.

Make evergreens the backbone of your collection of pots; they will serve you well right through the year, disguising ugly corners, breaking up hard surfaces, and marking focal points. Let them stand alone or dress them with seasonal colour, such as bulbs and summer bedding.

Caption clockwise from above: box (*Buxus sempervirens*) cones combined with trailing ivy; *Euonymus fortunei*
'Emerald 'n' Gold' with purple-leaved hazel (*Corylus avellana* 'Purpurea'); and *Ilex aquifolium*' Handsworth New Silver'.

In the winter garden it is particularly pleasing to have a fragrant plant that will lift your spirits on a gloomy day. The small-leaved, evergreen Christmas box (*Sarcococca hookeriana* var. *humilis*) has insignificant but highly scented white flowers along its stems. The winter-flowering honeysuckle (*Lonicera* x *purpusii*) is another perfumed favourite, but it needs a large pot for a good root run to do well.

Winter jasmine (*Jasminum nudiflorum*) is a bright choice for near the house. Its trailing stems can be tied into a trellis, or left to trail over the edge of a container. It provides a good base cover for early bulbs to peep through. Shrubs, such as *Skimmia rubella,* and many of the small-leaved hebes are also useful for strong colour and shape. Flowering shrubs, such as camellias, are also rewarding. They are stand-alones, providing all the ornament you need in their own foliage and shape, with breathtaking flowers in late winter.

Among my top winter container plants are evergreen herbs, in particular rosemary, sage, thyme, and bay. Sage has such variety of foliage colour: grey-green, purple and tri-coloured, although the last type is not reliably hardy in all areas.

Bay, too, has a variety of foliage - green, as well as a golden leaf form. The usual green type looks good shaped into pyramids or into round mop-head standards. Bay's formal look suits the front door, and at the festive season, red ribbons will give standards a holiday look. Hollies, especially those with golden or silvery variegations, are also sold as mop-head plants in containers. Festive treatment suits them too.

Winter ornamentals

Ornamental cabbages and kales, in combinations of pinks, greys, green, and white, deepen in colour as the temperature lowers. You can spray glitter onto their foliage rims to give them a festive look, but they make such a splash of colour that they hardly need gilding or silvering.

Heathers and dwarf conifers will provide colour and shape, whatever the weather. In spring you can move the heathers out and replace them with spring bedding plants.

Ornamental grasses, such as *Festuca glauca*, with its blue-grey

OPPOSITE
Glazed pots holding bronzed sedges including *Carex dipsacea* and amber-and-purple foliage heucheras (*Heuchera* x *brizoides* 'Can-can' and *H.* 'Amber Waves') glow like burnished copper against the gravel patio through the winter.

ABOVE
Evergreen climbers such as ivy will survive the frost, and New Zealand flax also proves to be frost hardy.

foliage, and strappy-leaved plants, such as *Ophiopogon nigrescens* look good on their own. Plant early flowering bulbs around them and they will provide a strong background for the bulbs in spring.

In mild periods in late winter and early spring, look at the overall shape of any permanent plantings you have in containers of deciduous trees and shrubs. This is the time to prune out any dead, damaged, or diseased wood, and shape them lightly. But don't do this if frost is forecast.

Once frosts occurs, it is the testing time to see if your containers are indeed frost-proof. Bulbs, such as snowdrops, *Iris reticulata*, and winter

aconites, planted in autumn, will provide you with colour in late winter.

You will still need to protect non-hardy plants from the combined effects of frost, and cold, water-logged compost. Check that all the coverings, whether they are plastic, fleece, or plant branches, are still securely in place. If frost is forecast, and you have removed any protection during periods of warmer weather, replace it as soon as possible.

If you have greenhouse facilities or a location inside where you can provide a minimum temperature of 16°C (61°F), you can sow sweet pea seeds, as well as many other seeds for your summer containers.

ABOVE LEFT
Hydrangeas are excellent summer container plants, but they need a great deal of water. In winter don't cut back the spent flower stems: they will continue to look good, especially if frosted.

ABOVE
The Lenten rose *(Helleborus orientalis)* and winter-flowering pansies make a rich velvety combination in a terracotta wall pot.

OPPOSITE
On a winter's day, *Phormium cookianum* 'Maori Chief' offers its own rays of sunshine.

winter colour

plants

- *Ilex aquifolium* 'Silver Milkmaid'
- *Skimmia japonica* 'Rubella'
- Ornamental cabbage
- *Hedera helix* 'Glacier'
- Heathers
- *Skimmia japonica* ssp. *reevesiana*
- *Euphorbia amygdaloides* 'Purpurea'
- *Mahonia* x *wagneri* 'Undulata'
- *Brachyglottis monroi*

plant alternatives

- Golden bay
- *Choisya ternata* 'Sundance'
- Other variegated hollies
- Cyclamen
- *Euonymus* 'Emerald 'n' Gold'
- *Heuchera* 'Palace Purple'

MATERIALS

- Three terracotta containers of various shapes and sizes
- Drainage material (crocks, polystyrene, gravel)
- Loam-based compost

Even in winter your container collection can glow with colour from foliage, berries, and flowers. By choosing the shrubs, trees, and flowering plants that have the best and brightest foliage and blooms, you can create pots that will offer long-term colour.

In the large pot at the back of this planting, a specimen tree, one of the variegated hollies, *Ilex aquifolium* 'Silver Milkmaid', provides wavy green foliage with a central blotch of cream. If you have male hollies in the vicinity, it will also produce scarlet berries. In the garden this slow-growing holly would grow to 5.5m (18ft), but the container will restrict its height. It is best grown on its own as a specimen plant, so that its dense shape can develop well.

The conifers and heathers are best treated as temporary and seasonal additions to the holly pot. Leave them in the containers they came in and make a well in the compost of the main pot for them to nestle into just inside it. Cover them with compost and add a decorative mulch.

In the smaller pot, the purple of the foliage and flowering plants is offset by trails of variegated ivy. In the centre and at the back are two evergreen shrubs, with woodspurge (*Euphorbia amygdaloides* 'Purpurea') in the front. *Skimmia japonica's* flowers bud up in winter and open into small pink clusters in spring. *Mahonia* x *wagneri* 'Undulata' has holly-like leaves that turn from green to purple-bronze in winter, with long sprays of yellow flowers in spring. The mahonia deserves its own container or planting out into the garden as it matures, and the woodspurge is best treated as a winter-only subject as it spreads vigorously, and would soon overwhelm other plants.

The smallest pot in the foreground needs eye-catching plants to make it the main attraction. Ornamental cabbages are the perfect winter bedding to achieve this. They are available from garden centres, or you can grow your own from seed, sown in summer and planted up in autumn. As the temperatures reduce in winter, their colouring deepens. They are available in a variety of leaf shapes and colours, ranging from candy pink through to regal purple, and the snow-white of this collection.

In the small pot the cabbages are teamed with variegated trailing ivy and the red-berried *Skimmia japonica reevesiana*. At the back of this pot is a frost-hardy shrub, *Brachyglottis monroi*, whose silvery-grey foliage adds to the festive look of the collection. In spring it produces yellow flowers, which don't always seem to go well with its foliage.

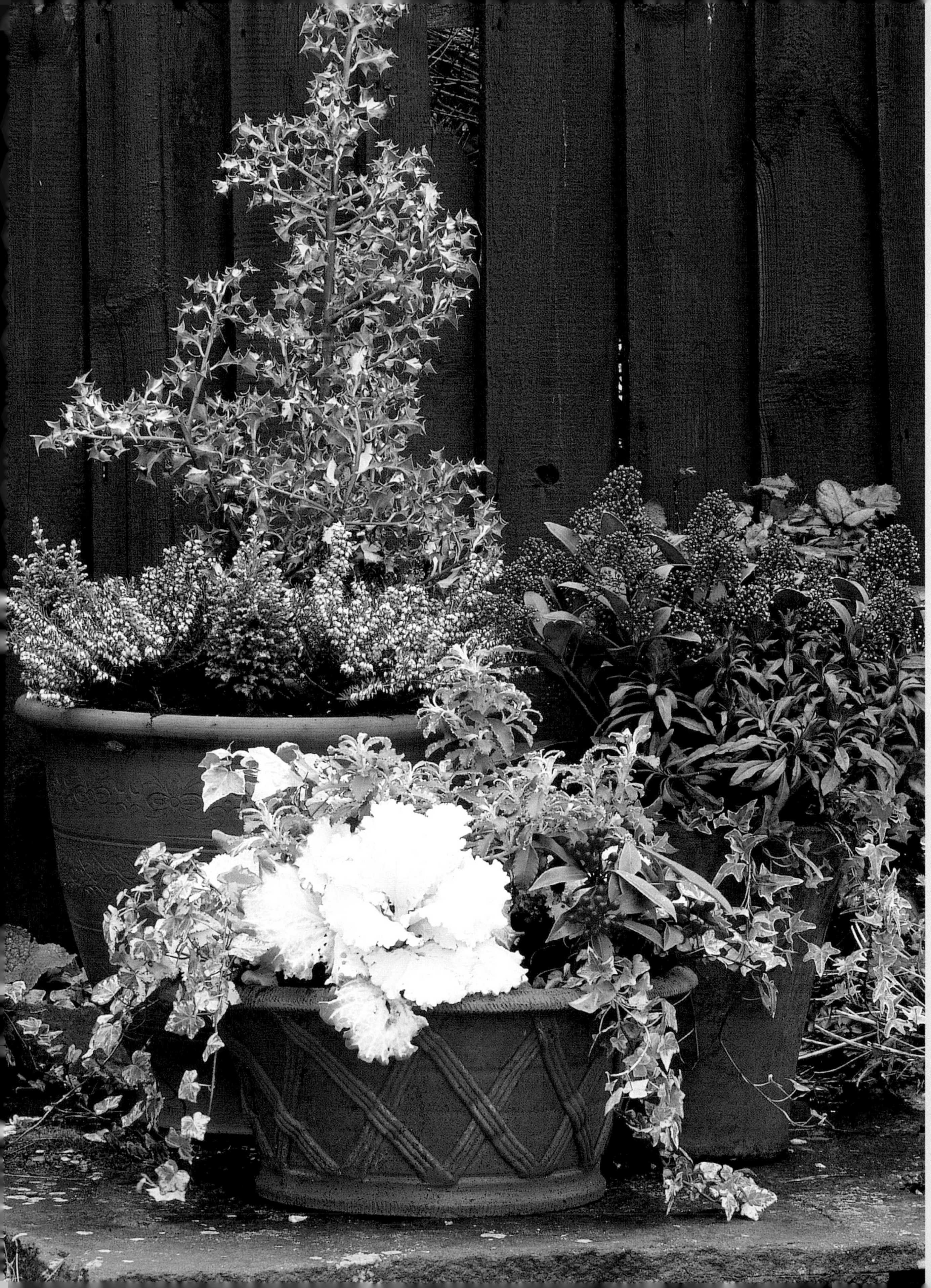

winter evergreens

plants
- *Pinus mugo*
- *Stipa arundinaria*
- *Carex buchananii*

plant alternatives
- *Juniperus chinensis* 'Obelisk'
- *Taxus baccata* (Yew)
- *Chamaecyparis lawsoniana* 'Aurea Densa'
- *C. obtusa* 'Nana Gracilis'
- *Cryptomeria japonica* 'Vilmoriniana'
- *Stipa tenuissima*
- Various bamboos

MATERIALS
- Three terracotta pots of similar size
- Ericaceous compost for both spruces and pines
- Loam-based compost for most trees and shrubs
- Drainage material (crocking, polystyrene, gravel)

Needing little maintenance but nonetheless offering style, colour, texture, and shape, there is nothing to beat permanent plantings of evergreen specimen plants. Conifers, small trees, and shrubs, and grasses are among the top container choices to fulfil this role.

There are many slow-growing and dwarf conifers that can be grown in pots, and will take years before they need to be planted out in the garden. The compact dwarf mountain pine (*Pinus mugo*) is a perfect choice. It is also available in a form that turns golden yellow in autumn, *P. mugo* 'Winter Gold'. 'Humpy' is a compact variety that grows into a mounded bright-green bush.

Conifers, small trees, and evergreen shrubs are best grown as single plants in the container. Pines and spruces prefer lime-free compost, so they will be simple to grow on their own. Some conifers, trees and shrubs, such as yew, box and bay, can be topiarized into attractive shapes. When planting these specimen trees and shrubs make sure they have good drainage and add a slow-release fertiliser to the compost when you are potting them up.

Other useful conifers are the dwarf golden cypress, *Chamaecyparis lawsoniana* 'Aurea Densa', or, with feathery foliage, the conical-shaped cypress, *Chamaecyparis obtusa* 'Nana Gracilis'. The conical *Juniperus chinensis* 'Obelisk' has attractive grey-blue foliage. For good autumn and winter colour the dwarf Japanese cedar, *Cryptomeria japonica* 'Vilmoriniana' turns from its summer green to a coppery russet in autumn after a few cold nights, and keeps its colour through the winter.

When you are planning what other pots and plants to combine with your specimen conifers, trees, and shrubs, try to visualize how these plants will look together. It is almost as if you are looking at opposites, the Yin and Yang of how the plants will harmonize with each other.

In this grouping, two grasses – also excellent choices in the low-maintenance stakes – work well with the evergreen conifer. The fountain-like shape of *Stipa arundinaria* fans out, while the more upright shape of *Carex buchananii* adds a change of height to this otherwise low-growing group.

From late summer onwards the grasses lose the fresh tones of their spring foliage. As they mature, the foliage becomes a straw colour, making a good foil for the conifer. They don't need to be cut back; you can simply tease and comb the dead strands out to make way for the new growth in spring.

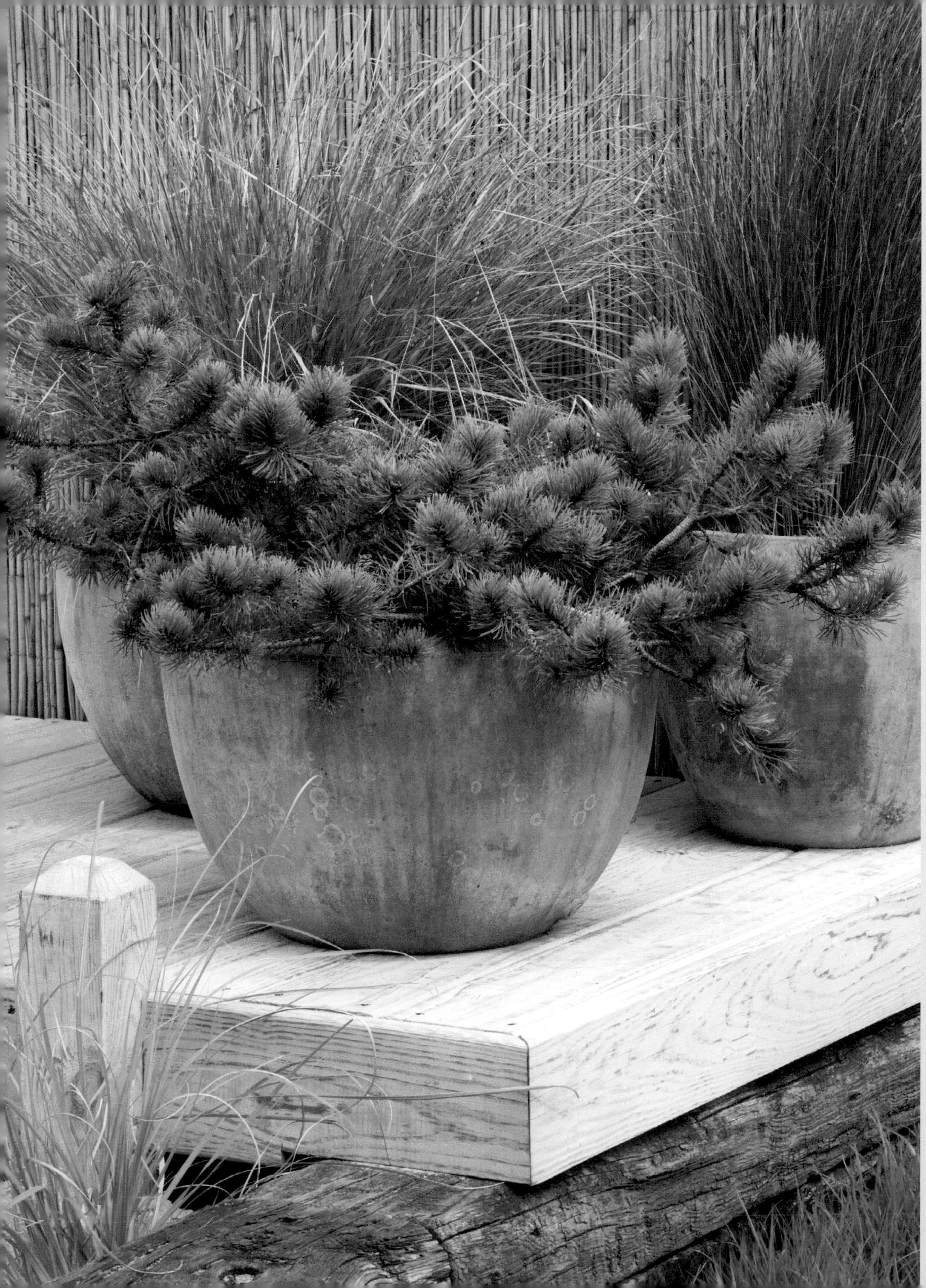

A–Z plant list

The Plant Directory

Most plants, given the appropriate conditions, will grow in containers. However, some plants are easier to maintain than others, putting up well with the extreme conditions that life in a pot can sometimes offer, especially if you are a less-than-perfect container gardener – drought, followed by flood, restricted roots, and shortage of soil and nutrients. The Plant Directory on the next few pages gives some examples of the easier and best-looking plants for containers – the ones that will need the minimum of care and attention to look really good in a pot.

Plants come in very many different species, varieties, cultivars, and hybrids, and new ones are being bred all the time. To recommend and describe particular plants, when in practice one variety may be exactly like another within the same species, would be unhelpful – a recipe for spending a frustrating time hunting for needles in haystacks, in fact. This section is therefore intended to point you in the direction of groups of plants to look out for when you visit a garden centre, nursery, or seed catalogue, so that you will read plant labels or ask more about them, to see if they will fit your requirements. For example, how big will it grow in a container, what colour are its flowers, and when do they appear?

Each entry names a plant or a generic group of plants (or sometimes a particular species), giving its common name where there is one. A very brief general description of the group follows, whether it is normally evergreen, and what other points of interest it might have, for example. The size that a plant will grow to when it spends its life in a pot will depend on many factors, such as the size of the pot, its position in sun or shade, how much you water, prune, and feed it. The heights given here, therefore, are a rough guide only, to help you find the plant to suit your needs. (For details of climate zones see p. 157.)

Shrubs

This group of plants include some invaluable evergreens that can provide an all-year backbone to your container garden. Plant them in loam-based compost or in ericaceous compost if they don't like lime (check the plant label). Pot them on into a bigger pot in spring if they grow too large in their existing containers, or carefully remove the top layer of compost and replace it with fresh compost if the plants have reached the biggest size you can accommodate. Add slow-release fertilizer granules to the new compost, and all you need to do to keep your shrub growing well is to water it, especially in dry weather, and prune if necessary.

Abutilon

Abutilon is a delightful perennial plant with attractive leaves and flowers throughout the summer. It comes in plain green, or variegated foliage with crimson, yellow, or orange bell flowers. It needs a sunny spot.
Season of interest: summer
Height: 60cm–1m (2–3ft)
Hardiness: Not reliably frost hardy. Zone 8

Berberis

Berberis darwinii has small yellow-to-orange flowers in summer, followed by blue berries. Its small evergreen, holly-like leaves are attractive all through the year. *B. thunbergii* is a thorny deciduous shrub that has several useful varieties. Purple-leaved 'Red Pillar' often turns scarlet in winter. The dwarf 'Atropurpurea Nana' makes a compact pot plant. Also has shiny red fruits in autumn. Berberis tolerates shade.
Season of interest: all year
Height: up to 2m (6ft)
Hardiness: Frost hardy. Zones 4–7

Camellia

Camellia japonica and *C.* x *williamsii* varieties and hybrids include some marvellous winter- and spring-flowering shrubs with handsome glossy evergreen leaves. Flowers are white, red, or pink, double or single depending on the variety you choose. Use lime-free ericaceous compost. Tolerates shade.
Season of interest: winter and spring
Height: up to 2m (6ft) or more
Hardiness: Frost hardy. Zones 7–9

Ceanothus

Ceanothus arboreus (California lilac) includes some really attractive spring-, summer-, and autumn-flowering shrubs. Some are evergreen and others deciduous. All have clusters of mainly blue, but some white or pink, flowers. Needs a sunny, sheltered spot.
Season of interest: early summer or autumn
Height: up to 2m (6ft)
Hardiness: Frost hardy. Zone 8

Choisya

Choisya ternata (Mexican orange) is a lovely mid-green, glossy-leaved evergreen with white scented flowers mainly in spring, though it may also flower at other times through the year too. Best in sun.

Season of interest: spring
Height: up to 2m (6ft)
Hardiness: Frost hardy. Zone 7

Cordyline

Cordyline australis (cabbage palm) is an evergreen, architechtural plant. It has dramatic sword-like evergreen leaves, which are green, purple, or variegated, depending on your choice. Tolerates light shade.

Season of interest: all year
Height: up to 2m (6ft)
Hardiness: Not reliably frost hardy. Zone 10

Cornus

Cornus alba (red-barked dogwood) makes a dramatic splash of colour in the winter months with its leafless stems. *C.sericea* 'Flaviramea' offers yellow-green stems. Needs pruning back every year, to get best display of coloured stems. Some have variegated leaves. Prefers sun

Season of interest: winter
Height: up to 2m (6ft)
Hardiness: Frost hardy. Zones 2–3

Corylus

Corylus avellana 'Contorta' (Corkscrew hazel) is a slow-growing deciduous shrub with twisted stems, large mid-green leaves in spring and summer and pretty yellow catkins in early spring. Medium to large shrub. 'Purpurea' is a dark maroon-leaved variety with straight (not contorted stems). Tolerates shade.

Season of interest: spring
Height: up to 2m (6ft)
Hardiness: Frost hardy. Zone 4

Erica

Erica carnea (winter heath) is particularly useful for winter flowers and foliage. Look for 'Springwood White' for white flowers or 'December Red' for dark pink blooms. Prefers sun.

Season of interest: winter
Height: 30cm (1ft)
Hardiness: Frost hardy. Zone 5

Euonymus

Euonymus fortunei is a useful ground covering, evergreen foliage shrub that can be clipped to form a low carpet. There are many different varieties, mostly with white (silver) or yellow (gold) variegated leaves – for example 'Emerald 'n' Gold' is bright green with yellow-splashed leaves. *E. japonicus* 'Microphyllus Pulchellus' is a compact variety. In cold weather the foliage may take on a reddish tinge. Spreading shrub. Tolerates shade.

Season of interest: all year
Height: 1.2m (4ft)
Hardiness: Frost hardy. Zones 5–7

Fuchsia

Fuchsias make great pot plants. Some have plain, small flowers, while others have large, colourful and very shapely blooms. *Fuchsia* 'Thalia' is not frost hardy. It has eye-catching elongated red flowers which, although not especially large, are produced in big clusters. Fuchsias are shade-tolerant. They grow tall if trained as standards.

Season of interest: summer
Height: 1m(3ft)
Hardiness: Some varieties are frost hardy. Zones 6–10

Gaultheria

Gaultheria mucronata is an evergreen bushy shrub with small, neat, dark green leaves. Choose a female variety 'Mulberry Wine' for its white flowers in spring and early summer followed by pink to rose-coloured berries. *G. procumbens* is compact and low-growing, and has white flowers and berries in autumn. Tolerates shade.

Season of interest: winter, spring and summer
Height: 1.2m (4ft)
Hardiness: Frost hardy, Zones 4–6

Hydrangea

Hydrangea macrophylla 'Hamburg' has large pink to deep mauve flowers, which fade attractively and stay on the plant through into autumn. Leave them on the plant for winter effects and to protect next year's buds from severe weather. Grow it in sun and water frequently.

Season of interest: summer to early winter
Height: 1.5–2m (5–6ft)
Hardiness: Frost hardy. Zones 5–10

Isoplexis

Isoplexis canariensis (Canary island foxglove) is an evergreen shrub with orange foxglove-like flowers in summer. It needs a sunny position and protection from frost.

Season of interest: summer
Height: up to 1.5 (5ft)
Hardiness: Not frost hardy. Zone 9

Lavandula

Lavandula (lavender) comes in several different species and many varieties. English *Lavandula angustifolia* and its varieties are hardier than the French *Lavandula stoechas*. Most have greyish-green foliage topped in summer by spikes or blue, purple, mauve or white flowers depending on the variety. Small to medium shrub. All lavenders prefer a sunny position and dislike wet conditions, especially in winter.

Season of interest: summer
Height: 60cm (2ft)
Hardiness: Most are frost hardy. Zones 5–9

Lonicera

Lonicera purpusii is a semi-evergreen large shrub with fragrant cream-coloured flowers in winter, followed by small red berries. Tolerates some shade.

Season of interest: winter and spring
Height: 1.8m (6ft)
Hardiness: Frost hardy. Zone 6

Pieris

Pieris formosa is an evergreen bushy shrub with large dark green leaves. *P. Japonica* 'Forest Flame' has cluster of white flowers in spring and its new leaves are bright red in spring. Tolerates shade.

Season of interest: spring
Height: up to 2m or more (6ft)
Hardiness: Frost hardy. Zones 6–7

Rhododendron

Rhododendrons come in many different species and varieties. Flower colours range from white, yellow, orange, red, and purple. Typically they are large dark-green evergreen shrubs with flowers in late spring or early summer. Azaleas are a group of dwarf deciduous rhododendron varieties and hybrids with very colourful, sometimes scented flowers. All rhododendrons are best grown in lime-free ericaceous compost. Tolerates shade.

Season of interest: spring
Height: up to 2m or more(6ft)
Hardiness: Frost hardy. Zones 4–9

Rosa

Rosa (roses) come in very many shapes, sizes, and flower colours, scented or unscented. Patio rose varieties have been especially bred to grow in containers. Some rose varieties are grafted and grow as standards, for example, 'Amber Queen', which look great in a pot. Roses are deciduous and flower from early summer. Some varieties carry on flowering until the autumn frost. Needs sun.

Season of interest: summer
Height: up to 2m (6ft)
Hardiness: Frost hardy. Zones 4–9

Rosmarinus

Rosmarinus officinalis (rosemary) is an attractive thin-leaved evergreen woody herb with bright-blue flowers in early summer. 'Miss Jessops Upright' is a more upright-growing variety. There are forms with pink or white flowers. Needs a sunny position.

Season of interest: early summer
Height: up to 1.5m (5ft)
Hardiness: Frost hardy. Zone 6

Salvia

Salvia officinalis (sage) has soft, grey-green evergreen foliage. Choose from many variegated varieties with cream-, purple-, or red-tinged leaves. This culinary herb has blue-mauve or white flowers in summer. Needs a sunny position.

Season of interest: all year
Height: up to 1m (3ft)
Hardiness: Frost hardy. Zones 6–9

Sarcococca

Sarcococca confusa (Christmas box) is an evergreen shrub grown for its sweet-smelling winter flowers and black fruits. *S. confusa* is also suitable. Tolerates shade.

Season of interest: winter
Height: 1.5m (5ft)
Hardiness: Frost hardy. Zone 6

Skimmia

Skimmia japonica is a dense evergreen shrub with mid-green leaves and strongly scented white spring flowers. If both male and female plants are grown, then red berries are produced on female plants. *S. j. reevesiana* is both male and female on one plant. 'Rubella' is a male variety whose flowers are pink in bud in winter then open pinkish-white in spring. Tolerates shade.

Season of interest: winter and spring
Height: up to 1.5m (5ft)
Hardiness: Frost hardy. Zone 7

Thymus

Thymus (thyme) comes in many species and varieties of different sizes and habits with plain green or variegated leaves. Prostrate thyme is useful for ground covering, while others like lemon thyme make an attractive small shrub. All thymes are best in a sunny position.

Season of interest: spring
Height: up to 60cm (2ft)
Hardiness: Most are frost hardy. Zones 5–9

Viburnum

Viburnum tinus is a dark-green evergreen shrub with clusters of white flowers during the winter months. It also has attractive dark berries. Tolerates shade.
Season of interest: winter
Height: up to 2m (6ft)
Hardiness: Frost hardy. Zone 7

Trees

Give your collection of pots some height by growing some small containerized trees. Evergreens offer the opportunity for foliage colour and texture in winter, when other plants are less showy or have disappeared underground! Many of the evergreen plants recommended here are good topiary plants – they can be snipped into any shape you fancy. Having one or two of these living sculptures will bring another design element to your garden, whether it is stately-home style, a modern, minimalist look, or may be just a spot of garden humour that you want. Some trees listed lose their leaves in autumn, but are recommended because their spring, summer, and autumn foliage is worth having. Whether you clip your potted trees into peacock shapes or leave them to grow, unhindered, you will need to be sure that they are sheltered from strong winds and that your pots are strong and solid, since trees, especially those grown as "standards", may be "top heavy" and can be blown over.

Acer

Acer palmatum (Japanese maple) includes many varieties and cultivars with more or less finely cut deciduous leaves in green (such as *A. p.* 'Ozakazuki') or purple (such as *A. p.* 'Atropurpurea'). Leaves of most of them turn scarlet or yellow in autumn. These make stunning miniature trees with ancient-looking gnarled stems. Needs a sheltered site and tolerates light shade.
Season of interest: spring, summer, and autumn
Height: up to 2m (6ft)
Hardiness: Frost hardy. Zone 5

Betula

Betula utilis (Himalayan birch) is a lovely tree with attractive white bark. It has delicate green foliage, which turns yellow in autumn, and small yellow catkins in spring. Needs a sunny position.
Season of interest: all year
Height: up to 2m (6ft)
Hardiness: Frost hardy. Zone 7

Buxus

Buxus sempervirens (box) is a small-leaved evergreen plant that is a favourite species for topiary. Its size depends on pruning, pot size, and variety. It grows best in sun or light shade.
Season of interest: all year
Height: up to 2m (6ft)
Hardiness: Frost hardy. Zone 5

Chamaerops

Chamaerops humilis (dwarf fan palm) has large evergreen fan-shaped fronds, arching away from its hairy trunk. Best grown in sun.
Season of interest: all year
Height: up to 2m (6ft)
Hardiness: Moderately frost hardy. Zone 9

Citrus

Citrus species and varieties (oranges, lemons etc) make lovely standard trees with glossy evergreen leaves and scented white flowers on and off through the year, and, of course, fruit. Grows best in sun or light shade, in a sheltered spot.
Season of interest: all year
Height: up to 2m (6ft)
Hardiness: Not frost hardy. Zone 9

Ilex

Ilex aquifolium and *I.* x *altaclerensis* varieties (holly) makes a very useful and attractive clipped cone or standard tree. *I. a. quifolium* 'Handsworth New Silver' has good variegated foliage and can be shaped into cones, standards, and even tiers. Holly leaves are plain green or variegated with white, cream, or yellow markings. Female varieties produce red orange or yellow berries in autumn when grown near to a male plant. Tolerates shade. Size depends on pruning.
Season of interest: all year
Height: up to 2m (6ft)
Hardiness: Frost hardy. Zone 6

Juniperus

Juniperus (junipers) are conifers that include upright, spreading- and ground-covering species, hybrids, and varieties. Many are slow-growing. *Juniperus communis* 'Compressa' is dwarf and upright, *J.c.* 'Prostrata' grows to form a spreading carpet-like cover. Shade tolerant.
Season of interest: all year
Height: up to 2m (6ft)
Hardiness: Frost hardy. Zones 2–7

Laurus

Laurus nobilis (bay) is an invaluable evergreen that can be trained to grow as a shaped tree (standards or cones are traditional) or kept as a bush. Use the leaves as a cooking herb. Prefers a warm, sheltered position; tolerates some shade.
Season of interest: all year
Height: up to 2m (6ft)
Hardiness: Frost hardy. Zone 8

Paulownia

Paulownia tomentosa (foxglove tree) is a deciduous tree with large, attractive, mid-green leaves. It will make a tall tree in a pot, though it may not flower. It is often grown solely for its foliage, in which case it is cut back or stooled annually. Needs a sunny position.
Season of interest: summer
Height: up to 2m (6ft)
Hardiness: Frost hardy. Zone 5

Pinus

Pinus mugo (dwarf pine) is a spreading conifer with bright-green to dark-green needles and brown cones. Prefers sun.
Season of interest: all year
Height: up to 2m (6ft)
Hardiness: Frost hardy. Zone 3

Trachycarpus

Trachycarpus fortunei (windmill palm) has large exotic-looking, fan-like evergreen leaves radiating from a single trunk. Best grown in a sunny position. It may be moderately hardy in the ground but in containers needs frost protection.
Season of interest: all year
Height: up to 2m (6ft)
Hardiness: Not frost hardy. Zone 9

Climbers

Using climbing plants in pots opens up the possibility of covering walls or trellis work, or clothing patio features, such as gazebos and pergolas. Climbers can also be useful to give an arrangement of several pots a bit of height, though a support will be necessary; the lax stems of a climber mean that it can tumble, flop, or cascade from a pot or, given a support, clamber upwards to give height to an arrangement, or screen a view.

Clematis

Clematis grow well in containers. There are very many different ones to choose from – winter-flowering, evergreen, small, and large-flowered – so be sure to check the label and keep it when you buy clematis, since different varieties prefer different methods of pruning. *Clematis florida* 'Sieboldii' has fascinating white summer flowers with prominent purple stamens. Most clematis prefer sun, but a few will tolerate some shade. Mostly they do well if their roots are shaded and therefore in the cool.
Season of interest: spring, summer, or autumn
Height: up to 2m (6ft)
Hardiness: Frost hardy. Zones 6–9

Cobaea

Cobaea scandens (cup and saucer vine) is a tendril climber with large bell-flowers that open cream and turn purple as they age. Can be grown as an annual. Requires sun.
Season of interest: summer
Height: up to 2m (6ft)
Hardiness: Not frost hardy. Zone 9

Hedera

Hedera helix (ivy) is an invaluable evergreen container plant. Whether you train it up a support or let it trail down to cover the pot, there's a useful job among your pots for at least one of its many varieties – plain green, large-leaved, or splashed with white, cream, or yellow. Ivy grows well in sun or shade.
Season of interest: all year
Height: up to 2m (6ft)
Hardiness: Most are frost hardy. Zone 5

Ipomea

Ipomea purpurea (morning glory) is an annual climber with twining stems. Flowers range from red, purple pink, or blue, depending on the variety. *I. lobata* has amber, orange, and cream flowers in clusters, while *I. batatas* is grown for its purple-bronze or citrine-gold foliage. *I. batatas* 'Blackie' has rich dark foliage. Needs sun.
Season of interest: summer
Height: up to 2m (6ft)
Hardiness: Some are frost hardy. Zones 7–9

Jasminum

Jasminum (jasmine) comes in summer- and winter-flowering forms. Choose *Jasminum nudiflorum* for bright yellow flowers in winter, and *J.officinale* for scented white flowers in summer. jasmines prefer a sunny position.
Season of interest: summer and winter
Height: up to 2m (6ft)
Hardiness: Most are frost hardy. Zones 6–7

Lathyrus

Lathyrus (sweet pea) has perennial (*Lathyrus latifolius*) and annual

(*L. odoratus*) species. Both are useful summer-flowering climbers. Perennial sweet pea has mauve-purple, pink, white, or bi-colour flowers, depending on species and variety. Annual sweet peas come in many delightful colours. All require sun.
Season of interest: summer
Height: up to 2m (6ft)
Hardiness: Frost hardy. Zones 4–10

Rhodochiton
Rhodochiton atrosanguineum is a fabulous and exotic climber with heart-shaped leaves and long, tubular, dark-red flowers in summer.
Season of interest: summer
Height: up to 2m (6ft)
Hardiness: Not frost hardy. Zones 9–10

Thunbergia
Thunbergia alata (black-eyed Susan) has pretty orange, black-centred flowers in summer. It is an annual climber that can be used for height with supports, or allowed to trail over the rim of a pot.
Season of interest: summer
Height: up to 2m (6ft)
Hardiness: Not frost hardy. Zone 10

Bulbs, corms, and tubers
Bring some character to your pots at any time of year with a seasonal show of bulbs, corms, and tubers. Many of these species have a somewhat short-lived flowering period, so be prepared to lift or move them somewhere out of sight when they have finished, and let them die back naturally. Replace bulb vacancies with different bulb species or varieties, or fill in the spaces with other temporary plants such as bedding plants.

Allium
Allium karataviense is among several beautiful ornamental onions. This one has a low-growing, pinkish, globe-shaped flower that nestles amongst its distinctive large blue-green leaves in late spring. It prefers a sunny position. *A. moly* is low-growing, has yellow flowers and flourishes in sun.
Season of interest: late spring
Height: 15–30cm (6in–1ft)
Hardiness: Frost hardy. Zones 7–8

Anemone
Anemone blanda comes in pink, white, or blue varieties. It flowers in early spring with pretty, daisy-ike flowers. *A.* 'De Caen' hybrids are also good in containers. All tolerate shade.
Season of interest: spring
Height: 15cm (6in)
Hardiness: Frost hardy. Zones 5–8

Begonia
Begonias divide into several groups – the larger-flowered tuberous ones make particularly marvellous plants for pots. They have attractive foliage and huge blowsy blooms in bright colours. Begonias will grow in partial shade. *B.* 'Dragon's Wing' and *B.* 'Bonfire' are particularly good, with abundant flowers and showy foliage. One or two species are frost hardy, including *Begonia grandis* ssp *evansiana*.
Season of interest: summer
Height: 15–60cm (6in–2ft)
Hardiness: Most are not frost hardy. Zones 6–10

Canna
Canna indica (canna lilies) make stunning pots plants. They have large leaves with a variety of colour and markings that sheath a dramatic spike of colourful summer flowers. Bloom colours are scarlet, orange, or yellow depending on the variety. They need a sunny situation.
Season of interest: summer
Height: 1m (3ft)
Hardiness: Not frost hardy. Zone 8

Colchicum
Colchicum autumnale (autumn crocus) are not true crocuses but have similar cup-shaped mauve or white flowers that mostly appear in the autumn, followed by their leaves in the spring. Prefers sun.
Season of interest: autumn
Height: 15cm (6in)
Hardiness: Frost hardy. Zone 5

Crocus
Crocus species and varieties add a splash of spring colour, coming in cream, yellow, and purple varieties. Crocus prefers a sunny situation.
Season of interest: spring
Height: 15 (6in)
Hardiness: Frost hardy. Zones 4–8

Cyclamen
Cyclamen have distinctive white, pink, or purple butterfly-like flowers with attractive marbled leaves. Species and varieties vary in their flowering time, size, and hardiness. Some are scented. *Cyclamen coum* is winter-flowering, *C. hederifolium* flowers in autumn.
Season of interest: summer, autumn, or winter

Height: 15cm (6in) or less
Hardiness: Some are frost hardy, some are not. Zones 6–11

Dahlia

Dahlias come in a magnificent range of flower colours, shapes, and sizes, some with dark-red foliage. They do require supporting to look their best, unless you choose a dwarf variety. They need a sunny position.

Season of interest: summer
Height: up to more than 2m (6ft)
Hardiness: Frost hardy. Zones 8–10

Fritillaria

Fritillaries are spring-flowering bulbs with very different-looking species and varieties *Fritillaria imperialis* (crown imperials) make a magnificent splash in spring, in orange, rust, or yellow. *F. meleagris* (snakeshead frittilary) is a delightful bulb with white- or purple-chequered bell-shaped flowers in spring

Season of interest: spring
Height: 15cm–1m(6in–3ft)
Hardiness: Frost hardy. Zones 4–9

Galanthus

Galanthus nivalis (snowdrop) offers welcome winter flowers. Choose from single or double varieties. Prefers sun or part-shade.

Season of interest: winter or spring
Height: up to about 15cm (6in)
Hardiness: Frost hardy. Zones 4–6

Gladiolus

Gladiolus are magnificent, often brightly coloured, summer-flowering corms. The flowers are arranged along upright spikes, with sword-shaped leaves. Many hybrids are available with flower colours varying from white, through pinks and reds to yellows. There are also different species, some with much smaller flowers. Gladiolus prefers sun. Some species, including *G. illyricus* and *G. tristis* are frost hardy.

Season of interest: summer
Height: 15cm–1.2m (6in-4ft)
Hardiness: Not all are frost hardy. Zones 6–10

Hippeastrum

Hippeastrums, also sold as amaryllis, are beautiful, large-flowered frost-tender bulbs. They are often grown indoors, but will grow outside in pots, too, once the frosts are over. White, pink, orange, and red varieties are available. They prefer sun or light shade.

Season of interest: late winter or early spring
Height: 15–60cm (6in–2ft)
Hardiness: Not frost hardy. Zone 11

Hyacinthus

Hyacinthus (hyacinth) varieties and hybrids are mostly heavily scented with a more or less dense flowerhead in spring. Colours vary from white through cream, pink, maroon, purple, and blue. Prefers a sunny situation.

Season of interest: spring
Height: 15–20cm (6–8in)
Hardiness: Frost hardy. Zones 5–9

Iris

Iris reticulata (netted iris) is an early spring-flowering bulb, with delightful purple, mauve, or blue flowers, depending on the variety. Needs sun.

Season of interest: early spring
Height: 15cm (6in)
Hardiness: Frost hardy. Zones 7–10

Lilium

Lilium (lilies) are fantastic bulbs for summer pots. Use them to replace your spring bulbs, once they're past their best. There are many species and varieties available. The regal lily, *Lilium regale*, is one of the best. Short-stemmed cultivars that look good in containers include the dwarf Oriental lily which you can obtain from catalogues in mixed colours (30–50cm/2½ft). 'Stargazer' grows to 75cm/2.5ft' and has a speckled throats and clearly lined petals. Each bulb produces many trumpet- shaped, mostly fragrant flowers in summer. Lilies in general prefer their bulbs to be shaded, but enjoy holding their heads in the sun.

Season of interest: early to late summer
Height: 30–200cm (12in–6ft) or more
Hardiness: Many are frost hardy. Zones 5–6

Muscari

Muscari species and varieties (grape hyacinths) have scented blue or white flowers in spring. They are best grown in a sunny spot.

Season of interest: spring
Height: 15cm (6in) or more
Hardiness: Frost hardy. Zones 4–7

Narcissus

Narcissus (daffodils) come in many different shapes, sizes, colours, and frost hardiness and they also vary in their time of spring flowering, bringing with it the chance to have a succession of narcissus in

bloom from early to late spring. 'Tete a Tete' is short-stemmed, has multi-headed flower stems with small yellow flowers. 'Carlton' has large yellow flowers, while 'Cheerfulness' has small yellow or white flowers. They do best in a sunny site.
Season of interest: spring
Height: 15cm–60cm(6in–2ft)
Hardiness: Frost hardy. Zones 4–10

Sternbergia
Sternbergia lutea is autumn-flowering with crocus-like yellow flowers with white blotches at the centre. The flower is scented. Prefers a sunny site.
Season of interest: spring or autumn
Height: 15cm (6in)
Hardiness: Frost hardy. Zone 6

Tulipa
Tulipa (tulips) are spring-flowering bulbs that vary enormously. You can get tiny little ones, tall ones, ones that flower in early spring, others that flower in late spring. Flower colour shapes and size vary as well as their colour. *Tulipa tarda* has small multi-headed yellow flowers early in spring. *T. turkestanica* is multi-flowered with white blooms in early spring, and *T. sprengeri* is tall and has red flowers late in spring. 'Peachblossom' is early flowering in the spring. 'Princess Irene' has orange flowers with purple, flame-like markings in mid-season and 'Abu Hassan' is red with a yellow edge, also blooming in mid-season. All prefer sun.
Season of interest: spring
Height: 15cm–1m (6in–3ft)
Hardiness: Frost hardy. Zones 5–9

Zantedeschia
Zantedeschia aethiopica (arum lily) is a shapely plant with stunning white, yellow, green, pink, or purple flowers in summer. Prefers sun or partial shade. Can grow at the water's edge.
Season of interest: summer
Height: 60cm–1m (2–3ft)
Hardiness: Not reliably frost hardy. Zones 8–10

Perennials
Some perennials make a good choice for a pot plant, being easy-care and reliable, as well as self-supporting (needing no staking) and attractive all year. Here are a few to try. Some of the best perennials for pots are not hardy but frost tender, so be sure to bring these ones inside in autumn and wait in the following year until early summer before leaving them outside again.

Agapanthus
Agapanthus are excellent container plants. They make clumps of evergreen (not hardy) and deciduous (hardy), strap-shaped leaves topped by stems of attractive globe-shaped blue or white flowers in summer. Headbourne hybrids are particularly free-flowering and hardy. Grow in a sunny position.
Season of interest: summer
Height: 60cm–1m (2–3ft)
Hardiness: Deciduous ones are frost hardy. Zones 7–10

Ajuga
Ajuga reptans, A. pyramidalis and other (bugle) varieties are very useful ground-covering perennials with blue spring flowers and variegated or bronze evergreen foliage. Shade tolerant.
Season of interest: all year
Height: 15cm (6in) taller when in flower
Hardiness: Frost hardy. Zone 6

Argyranthemum
Arygranthemum (chrysanthemum) species, varieties, and hybrids include some great daisy-type flowering plants that keep blooming for months on end. Try *C. frutescens* varieties or hybrids such as 'Jamaica Primrose'. They enjoy sun.
Season of interest: summer and autumn
Height: 30cm–1.2m (12in–4ft)
Hardiness: Most are not frost hardy Zone 9

Astelia
Astelia chathamica makes a bold clump of sword-like evergreen leaves. It needs a sunny spot in a sheltered position out of cold winds. Needs to be well-drained or its base will rot.
Season of interest: spring
Height: 60cm–1m (2–3ft)
Hardiness: Not reliably frost hardy. Zone 9

Begonias see bulbs, corms, and tubers

Brassica
Brassica (ornamental cabbage and kale) varieties come in several different leaf colours and textures, in combinations of green, red, white, cream, and purple. They prefer a sunny position.
Season of interest: summer to winter
Height: 30–60cm (1–2ft)
Hardiness: Frost hardy. Zones 7–9

Campanula

Campanula (bellflowers) are a very varied group of plants ranging from small cushions of purple, blue, or white summer flowers to tall spires. They can be frost tolerant or not – so take care to check the label. 'Bali', for example, will not cope with frost and should be brought indoors. Will grow in sun.

Season of interest: summer to autumn
Height: 15–30cm (6in–1ft)
Hardiness: some are frost hardy.
Zones 5–10

Canna lilies see bulbs, corms, and tubers.

Chamaemelum

Chamaemelum nobile (chamomile) 'Treneague' is a ground-covering, deliciously scented foliage plant that prefers a sunny position. *C. nobile* 'Flore Pleno' like Treneague is scented but has small white, double flowers in addition.

Season of interest: summer
Height: 15cm (6in)
Hardiness: Frost hardy. Zone 4

Dahlias see bulbs, corms, and tubers

Dianthus

Dianthus (carnations and pinks) hybrids are grey- or green-leaved summer-flowering plants that come in white, pinks yellows and orange. 'Pink Parfait' is a bright, low-growing variety. Flowers are scented.

Season of interest: summer
Height: 15cm–1m (6in–3ft)
Hardiness: Most are frost hardy. Zones 3–9

Diascia

Diascias are used as summer bedding but are in fact perennials that can be overwintered in a sheltered site in mild winters. Diascias flower over a long period from summer through to autumn and provide a mass of flowers that look as if they are dancing or shimmering in the air, blooming as they do on long thin stems, some of which are upright and others have a trailing, pendulous habit. They can be purchased as young plants. The flowers are white, pink, salmon-pink or apricot. Grows best in well drained soil in full sun. Deadhead as flowers fade.

Season of interest: summer through to autumn
Height: 15–30cm/ (6–12in)
Hardiness: Frost hardy. Zone 8

Ensete

Ensete ventricosum is an evergreen, exotic-looking foliage perennial with banana-like stature. Grows in sun or partial shade in acid soil or ericaceous compost. Overwinter it indoors.

Season of interest: summer
Height: up to or more than 2m (6ft)
Hardiness: Not frost hardy. Zone 10

Gaura

Gaura lindheimeri (butterfly plant) is a bushy plant with pink-tinged flowers in summer. Likes a sunny position.

Season of interest: summer
Height: 1.2m (4ft)
Hardiness: Frost hardy. Zones 2–9

Heuchera

Heuchera is an excellent evergreen ground-covering perennial with summer flowers in white or pink held on wiry stems above the green, purple, or amber foliage depending on the variety you choose. It will tolerate some shade.

Season of interest: all year
Height: 15cm–1m (6in–3ft)
Hardiness: Frost hardy. Zones 4–6

Hosta

Hostas are grown for their textured and coloured leaves in spring and summer (they are dormant in winter). Hosta foliage can be plain green, variegated, metallic grey, almost buttery golden, wavy-edged, or plain, small, or large. They have spikes of tubular flowers in summer. They tolerate shade. Grow them in a loam-based compost so they don't dry out and feed with high-nitrogen fertilizer frequently during the growing seasaon.

Season of interest: summer
Height: 15cm–1m (6in–3ft)
Hardiness: Frost hardy. Zones 3–10

Lotus

Lotus maculatus (parrot's beak) is an exotic-looking trailing plant with tawny, burnt-orange flowers in summer and feathery, but metallic-grey, foliage. *L. berthelotii* has similar foliage and red beak-like flowers. Requires sun.

Season of interest: summer
Height: 30cm (1ft)
Hardiness: Not fully frost hardy. Zones 8–9

Musa

Musa basjoo (Japanese banana) looks like a tree, but it is a herbaceous perennial that will regrow if cut back. It has large architectural foliage, which is much used in jungle-style plantings. Grow it in sun in

a well-drained compost with added grit. Feed with a high-nitrogen fertiliser in the growing season. Needs protection in winter.
Season of interest: spring to autumn
Height: 3–5m (9–15ft)
Hardiness: Not frost hardy. Zone 10–11

Osteospermum

Osteospermum (Cape daisy) grows to form a clump of evergreen greyish-green foliage. Its daisy-shaped flowers appear in summer. Flowers are white with blue backs, purple, creamy yellow, or pink depending on the variety. It needs a sunny position.
Season of interest: summer
Height: 15cm–1m (6in–3ft)
Hardiness: Some are not frost hardy. Zones 8–10

Pelargonium

Pelargonium (geranium) comes in many shapes and sizes. For container growing, ivy-leaved trailers are great. For a bushier plant choose regal or zonal varieties such as the 'Sensation' series. Flower colours are red, white, and pink, appearing in dense clusters. They grow best in full sun.
Season of interest: summer to autumn
Height: 15cm–1m (6in–3ft)
Hardiness: Not frost hardy. Zone 10

Phormium

Phormium (New Zealand flax) is an evergreen perennial that forms a large and dramatic clump of strap-shaped leaves. Varieties with different coloured leaves, plain and variegated, are available. These tall perennials need a sunny position.
Season of interest: All year

Height: Up to 2m (6ft) or more
Hardiness: Frost hardy. Zones 8–10

Primula

Primula hybrids (polyanthus primulas) are really two-year plants rather than permanent features. They come in a varied cheerful range of flower colours from white, through yellow, orange, red, and blue. They flower in late spring and early summer and require sun or partial shade.
Season of interest: spring
Height: 15cm–30cm (6in–1ft)
Hardiness: Frost hardy. Zones 6–9

Solenostemon

Solenostemon (coleus) are grown for their marvellous velvety, colourful foliage, in patterned combinations of dark red and green, yellow and green, purple and green and many other rich mixtures. This bushy plant grows in sun or partial shade.
Season of interest: summer
Height: 30cm–1m (1–3ft)
Hardiness: Not frost hardy. Zone 10

Zantedeschia aethiopica see bulbs, corms, and tubers

Ornamental grasses and bamboos

This is a distinctive group of perennial plants that can make excellent easy-going container plants. Their 'flowers' are usually foliage-coloured to creamy-beige and insignificant, so grasses are grown for the form, texture, colour, and size of their leaves. Even though the flowers are not significant the seedheads that follow them are highly attractive and a great bonus.

Acorus

Acorus gramineus (sweet flag) is a delightful semi-evergreen grass that enjoys moist conditions. 'Hakuro-nishiki', 'Variegatus', and 'Ozori' are all good varieties with different coloured variegation. 'Ogon' is variegated and makes a splash of cool colour in a hot-coloured collection of plants. Acorus forms a medium-sized clump that enjoys a sunny spot.
Season of interest: all year round
Height: 15cm (6in)
Hardiness: Frost hardy. Zone 5

Carex

Carex belong to a group of very attractive waterside sedge plants. They vary in leaf colour and variegation. *Carex buchananii, C. muskingumensis, C. comans,* and *C. ishimensis* 'Evergold' are all worth using in containers. Grow in a sunny position in moisture-retentive soil.
Season of interest: all year
Height: 1m (3ft) plus
Hardiness: Frost hardy. Zones 5–9

Fargesia

Fargesia murielae (umbrella bamboo) makes an attractive evergreen clump of arching leafy stems. It prefers a sunny position.
Season of interest: all year
Height: up to 2m (6ft) or more
Hardiness: Not reliably frost hardy. Zone 9

Festuca

Festuca glauca (blue fescue) makes an eye-catching tuft of bluish evergreen grass. Comes in different varieties, such as 'Elijah Blue'. Grow it in a sunny position.

Season of interest: all year
Height: 15–40cm (6–16in)
Hardiness: Frost hardy. Zones 4–8

Hakonechloa

Hakonechloa macra 'Alboaureola' is an arching tuft of green leaves striped with yellow. It grows well in a sunny position.
Season of interest: all year
Height: 75cm(2½ft)
Hardiness: Frost hardy. Zone 5

Ophiopogon

Ophiopogon planiscapus 'Nigrescens' (lilyturf) is an evergreen, ground-covering plant grown for its black grassy leaves. It also has attractive flowers. It likes sun or part shade.
Season of interest: all year
Height: 15–30cm (6in–1ft)
Hardiness: Frost hardy. Zone 6

Pennisetum

Pennisetum (fountain grass) grows to form a graceful mound of delicate arching foliage that needs a sunny position. *P. alopecuroides* and *P. orientale* are frost hardy, while others are not. *P.* 'Purple Majesty' is grown as an annual for its deep-purple foliage and seedheads.
Season of interest: summer
Height: 1–1.5m (3–5ft)
Hardiness: Frost hardy. Zones 7–9

Pseudosasa

Pseudosasa japonica (arrow bamboo) grows to form a magnificent clump of evergreen bamboo stems. It is a tall plant that can be used as screening on a balcony or patio. It prefers sun.
Season of interest: all year

Height: up to 2m (6ft)
Hardiness: Frost hardy. Zones 7–10

Stipa

Stipa arundinacea (pheasant grass) makes an elegant clump of arching foliage. Its seedheads catch the light and give the plant a liquid, fountain-like appearance. Prefers a sunny position.
Season of interest: summer and autumn
Height: up to 1.5m (5ft) or more
Hardiness: Frost hardy. Zone 8

Cacti/succulents

These fleshy-leaved plants mostly hail from warm, climates so bring them indoors for the winter. They usually like a sunny position and dislike standing in water – so provide good layers of drainage before you add compost and don't leave them in saucers of water.

Agave

Agave americana (century plant) makes a rosette of evergreen, sword-shaped sharply-pointed, grey-green leaves and dramatic tall white flowers in spring. Variegated varieties are available. Requires sun.
Season of interest: spring and summer
Height: 1m (3ft)
Hardiness: Not frost hardy. Zone 9

Echevaria

Echeveria are mostly small, succulent plants with a tight rosette of overlapping fleshy leaves. Need sun and shelter.
Season of interest: summer
Height: 15cm (6in)
Hardiness: Not frost hardy. Zone 8

Fascicularia

Fascicularia bicolor makes a flattened green rosette with an inner ring of red leaves and a central flower spike in summer. Needs sun.
Season of interest: summer
Height: 50cm (1½ft)
Hardiness: Not frost hardy. Zone 8

Sedum

Sedums (stonecrop) are a large and varied group of small succulent plants, often found in the rock garden or alpine section at garden centres. Make a collection of different species and varieties – or grow them singly in a pot. Needs sun.
Season of interest: summer and autumn
Height: 5–20cm (2–8in)
Hardiness: Some are frost hardy. Zones 7–9

Sempervivum

Sempervivum (houseleeks) are a great group of small succulents that will grow almost anywhere – even on the roof! They make dense rosettes of overlapping foliage and, when mature, produce pink flower-spikes in summer and make numerous off-sets. After flowering, individual small plants die off, but off-sets make for new generation of plants. Prefer sun.
Season of interest: summer
Height: 15cm (6in)
Hardiness: Frost hardy. Zones 4–7

Annuals

(and other temporary bedding plants)

This group includes some of our best-loved plants for pots. Annuals are sown and flower within a summer season. Some, treated as temporary plants, can be overwintered in shelter, or you can take cuttings from them for the next growing season. Either way, this is the group of plants on which to cut your container-gardening teeth. The effort you put in to them will be more than repaid in the flowers and foliage they produce right through the summer season. Since many of these plants don't live through winter, they are not all given climate zones. Here they are categorized as frost hardy or not frost hardy (seed catalogues sometimes use the term 'half-hardy' or 'tender', meaning that they will not survive a frost). Don't attempt to put plants that are not frost hardy outside until the danger of spring frosts has passed.

Arctotis
Arctotis is a South African plant with daisy-like flowers which come in white, cream, yellows and brown-reds. Prefers sun.
Season of interest: summer
Height: up to 60cm (2ft)
Hardiness: Not frost hardy. Zone 9

Arygranthemum
(chrysanthemum) see perennials

Bacopa
Bacopa 'Snowflake' has delightful little white flowers and tiny leaves – ideal for filling little gaps in pots and hanging baskets. *Bacopa* 'Baja' is a good alternative.
Season of interest: summer
Height: 15–25cm (6–10in)
Hardiness: Not frost hardy. Zone 8

Begonias see bulbs, corms, and tubers

Bidens
Bidens ferulifolia has tiny yellow star-flowers. It makes a spreading cushion that smothers the ground.
Season of interest: summer
Height: 15–30cm (6–12in)
Hardiness: Not frost hardy. Zone 8

Canna see bulbs, corms, and tubers

Cobaea see climbers

Gazania
Gazanias are drought-tolerant plants with colourful daisy flowers (in yellows, pinks, orange, and reds), with greyish green foliage. The 'Mini-star' series comprises compact and colourful plants. Need sun.
Season of interest: summer
Height: 15–20cm (6–12in)
Hardiness: Not frost hardy. Zones 2–9

Helichrysum
Helichrysum petiolare is a very useful foliage plant for pots. It has felted grey, rounded foliage carried on attractively branching stems. Makes a semi-trailing plant that prefers sun.
Season of interest: summer
Height: 30–60cm (1–2ft)
Hardiness: Not frost hardy. Zone 10

Impatiens
Impatiens walleriana (busy Lizzie) is a perennial, but is usually grown as an annual plant. It is available in mixed colour seed combinations or in single colour packs. The colour range includes white, violet, pink and lavender, as well as some with stripey markings. It blooms all through summer into the autumn with soft, flat, but open-faced flowers that appear to cover the entire plant. Grows equally well in sun or shade. You can also buy busy Lizzie as young plants.
Season of interest: summer to autumn
Height: up to 60cm/24in
Hardiness: Not frost hardy. Zone 10

Ipomea see climbers

Lathyrus see climbers

Lobelia
Lobelia erinus (lobelia) is a small but high-impact annual flowering plant with white, blue or mauve-pink flowers in summer, depending on variety. It is available as seed and as small plants. Some forms are very compact, and frothy while others have longer flowering stems that appear to cascade over the rims of pots. Grows best in full sun.
Season of interest: early summer through to autumn
Height: 10-23cm/4-9in
Hardiness: Half hardy. Zones 9-10

Lotus see perennials

Mimulus
Mimulus (monkey flower) has orange, red and yellow, plain or spotted flowers on

compact plants. Try the 'Malibu' series or 'Magic Spots'. *M. auriantiacus* is a shrubby plant that floats in and among others in a container collection. It has orange flowers. Grows well in partial shade.

Season of interest: summer
Height: 15–120cm (6in to 4ft)
Hardiness: Not frost hardy. Zones 6–8

Nemesia

Nemesias are annuals with lovely colourful, snap dragon-type flowers. 'National Ensign' is a very dramatic red and white one. 'Nebula Mixed' has amber, reds, and orange. Prefers sun.

Season of interest: summer
Height: 15–30cm (6–12in)
Hardiness: Not frost hardy

Osteospermum see perennials

Pelargonium see perennials

Petunia

Petunias give fantastic value for the summer months. Choose plain-coloured flower varieties in pinks, white, or purple, or veined, frilled, or bi-colours, doubles or singles on compact or trailing plants. Literally hundreds of varieties are available and new ones arrive all the time. Among many others, the 'Supercascade' and 'Surfinia' series are excellent. Will tolerate some shade.

Season of interest: summer
Height: 15–30cm (6–12in)
Hardiness: Not frost hardy

Solenostemon (see perennials)

Tropaeolum

Tropaeolum majus (nasturtium) is a vigorous climber or trailer with scarlet, orange, or yellow flowers. Dwarf varieties are more compact in habit, like 'Tip Top Ladybird'. Some varieties have bluish green leaves, for example 'Empress of India'. Some are variegated, like 'Alaska'. The flowers have a tendency to hide behind their leaves. Best in sun.

Season of interest: summer
Height: 30cm–1.2m (1–5ft)
Hardiness: Not frost hardy

Verbena

Verbena varieties, especially trailing verbena are very useful and attractive in pots, for example 'Quartz Waterfall' comes in shades of blue, lavender purple, and white. It makes a sprawling, low-growing plant that tolerates some shade.

Season of interest: summer
Height: 15–30cm (6–12in) or more
Hardiness: Not frost hardy. Zones 8–10

Viola

Viola (violas and pansies) species, varieties, and hybrids are very useful for pots. Their flowering season is long, many of them blooming right through winter, and they tolerate shade. Pansies have larger flowers and come in a very wide range of flower colours. Violas tend to be smaller flowered and more subtle in colourways. Treat as hardy annuals or as bi-ennials depending on variety.

Season of interest: autumn, winter, and spring
Height: 15–30cm (6–12in)
Hardiness: Frost hardy. Zones 4–10

Zaluzianskya

Zaluzianskya capensis (Cape night phlox) is a low-growing, spreading plant with white-to-pale-pink scented flowers.

Season of interest: summer
Height: 15–45cm (6–18in)
Hardiness: Not frost hardy. Zone 9

Fruit and vegetables

Though yields will not be as large as with vegetables and fruit grown in unrestricted soil, growing containerised crops can be very satisfying – and they look attractive too. Give them all a sheltered and sunny spot for the best results.

Apples are attractive trees but for successful container cultivation you need to choose one that is grafted on to 'dwarfing rootstock'. So check the label carefully when you buy. The columnar 'Ballerina' trees make good container plants.

Season of interest: spring and autumn
Height: up to 2m (6ft) or more
Hardiness: Frost hardy. Zone 7

Runner beans provide both ornament and tasty crops. They grow well in containers, provided you give them support in the shape of canes to grow up. They need copious water and high nitrogen fertilizer in the growing season. Sow seed direct into the containers in spring. Harvest from summer to autumn.

Season of interest: spring and summer
Height: over 2m (6ft)
Hardiness: Not hardy

Blueberries are small shrubs and can be made to fruit in containers, provided that you grow them in lime-free, ericaceous compost. 'Earliblue' and 'Toro' are good choices. They tolerate shade.
Season of interest: summer and autumn
Height: 1–2m (3–6ft)
Hardiness: Frost hardy. Zone 2

Cabbages are great-looking plants for pots. Choose a red cabbage such as 'Monte Christo' or the green and purple-tinged 'Holly'. See also brassica in perennials.
Season of interest: summer and autumn
Height: 15–30cm (6–12in)
Hardiness: Frost hardy

Lettuce can look very pretty – either growing with other plants or in a pot on its own. Cut-and-come-again varieties are the most worthwhile. Choose a mixed variety such as 'Salad Bowl' for red and green leaves in one packet. Needs sun.
Season of interest: summer and autumn
Height: 15–30cm (6–12in)
Hardiness: Not frost hardy

Oriental leaves come in many different forms, some hot and peppery others cool and crisp. Best grown in the sun.
Season of interest: summer and autumn
Height: 15–30cm (6–12in)
Hardiness: Some are frost hardy

Potatoes need a deep pot to get a good-sized yield. Choose an early variety such as 'Mimi' for delicious salad potatoes. Best grown in sun.
Season of interest: summer
Height: 15–30cm (6–12in)
Hardiness: Not frost hardy

Strawberries are very useful container plants – especially the tiny-fruited alpine varieties.
Season of interest: summer
Height: 15–30cm (6–12in)
Hardiness: Frost hardy

Sweet peppers can do well in pots. Choose a dwarf variety with small fruits for the best results, for example 'Mini Sweet'. Needs sun.
Season of interest: summer and autumn
Height: 20cm–1m (18in–3ft)
Hardiness: Not frost hardy

Tomatoes make excellent pot plants – especially the small-fruited cherry tomatoes such as 'Tumbler', which has the bonus of being a small, compact plant which trails prettily. Needs sun.
Season of interest: summer and autumn
Height: 20cm–2m (4in–6ft)
Hardiness: Not frost hardy

Climate zones

As a guide to whether a plant will thrive in a particular climate, a zoning system has been devised by the United States Department of Agriculture. It is based on the average annual minimum temperature of an area. Most plants can be grown in several zones. The important thing to know is whether a plant can tolerate frost (below Zone 9). If it can't, either wrap it up when the weather is close to this temperature or bring it indoors until early summer.

Zone		
1	below −50°F	below −5.5°C
2	−50 to -40°F	−45.50 to −40.1°C
3	−40 to -30°F	−40.0 to −34.5°C
4	−30 to -20°F	−34.4 to −28.9°C
5	−20 to -10°F	−28.8 to −23.4°C
6	−10 to 0°F	−23.3 to −17.8°C
7	0 to +10°F	−17.7 to −12.3°C
8	+10 to +20°F	−12.2 to −6.7°C
9	+20 to +30°F	−6.6 to −1.2°C
10	+30 to +40°F	−1.1 to +4.4°C
11	over 40°F	over +4.4°C

Index

Acknowledgments

The author would like to thank Susanna Longley for her help in compiling the Plant A–Z.

Thanks are due in addition and especially to Gisela Mirwis for her research, checking, invaluable suggestions, criticism, support, and keen-eyed attention to detail.

PHOTOGRAPHIC ACKNOWLEDGMENTS
Clive Nichols and the Publishers would like to give particular thanks to Clare Matthews who planted up several containers specially for this book

Front cover: Clive Nichols/Chelsea 2001/Carole Vincent/Blue Circle;
Back cover, top left: Clive Nichols/Privett Garden Products;
Back cover, top right: Clive Nichols/ Chelsea 2000/Stephen Woodhams;
Back cover, bottom:Clive Nichols/Pettifers Garden, Oxfordshire

1 Clive Nichols/Clare Matthews; 2 Clive Nichols/Keukenhof Gardens, Holland; 5 Clive Nichols/Chelsea 2002/David Rosewarne; 7 Clive Nichols/Landscape; 8 Clive Nichols/ Wingwell Nursery, Rutland; 11 Clive Nichols/Hall Farm, Lincolnshire; 12-13 Clive Nichols/Hampton Court 2005/Fran Forster; 14-15 Clive Nichols/Chelsea 1995/Designer: Mark Walker; 16 Clive Nichols/Amir Schlesinger/My Landscapes; 17 top Clive Nichols/ Mark Pedro de la Torre; 17 bottom Clive Nichols/Pettifers, Oxfordshire; 18 Clive Nichols/Clare Matthews; 19 Clive Nichols/Chelsea 2001/Carole Vincent/Blue Circle; 20 Clive Nichols/Pettifers, Oxfordshire; 21 Clive Nichols/Chelsea 2005/Designer: David Domoney; 22 Clive Nichols/Wynniatt-Husey Clarke; 23 top Clive Nichols/Keukenhof Gardens, Holland; 23 bottom Clive Nichols/Charlotte Sanderson; 24 Clive Nichols/ Design by Bright Green; 25 Clive Nichols/Chelsea 1999/Design: Michael Balston; 26 Clive Nichols/Chelsea 2001/Andy Sturgeon/Circ Garden; 27 Clive Nichols; 28 Clive Nichols/Stephen Woodhams; 29 Clive Nichols/Wynniatt-Husey Clarke; 30 Clive Nichols /Hampton Court 2005/Adrian

Whittle; 31 Clive Nichols; 32-33 Clive Nichols/Joe Swift; 34 Clive Nichols/Chelsea 2003/Design: James Dyson & Jim Honey; 35 left Clive Nichols /Wynniatt-Husey Clarke; 35 right Clive Nichols/The Postern, Sussex; 36 left Clive Nichols; 36 right Clive Nichols/Catriona McLean; 37 Clive Nichols/Chelsea 2001/Carole Vincent/Blue Circle; 38-39 Clive Nichols/Charlotte Sanderson; 40 Clive Nichols/Claire Mee; 41 Clive Nichols; 42-43 Clive Nichols/Hampton Court 2005/Andrea Lowe; 44-45 Clive Nichols; 46 Clive Nichols/Jonathan Baillie; 47 left Clive Nichols; 47 right Clive Nichols/Pettifers, Oxfordshire; 48-49 Clive Nichols/Design by Bright Green; 50 Clive Nichols/Ralph Cade/Robin Green; 51 Clive Nichols/Chelsea 2001/Carole Vincent/Blue Circle; 52 Clive Nichols/Ralph Cade/Robin Green; 53 Clive Nichols/Tony Ridler; 54 Clive Nichols/Hampton Court 1996/David Stevens; 55 Clive Nichols/Woodchippings, Northamptonshire; 56 Clive Nichols/Swinton Lane, Worcestershire; 57 Clive Nichols/Louise & Nick Elliot; 58 Clive Nichols/Keukenhof Gardens, Holland; 59 Clive Nichols; 60-61 Clive Nichols/Launa Slatter; 62 Clive Nichols/Keukenhof Gardens, Holland; 63 Clive Nichols; 64-65 top Clive Nichols/Keukenhof Gardens, Holland; 65 bottom Clive Nichols/Clare Matthews; 66 Clive Nichols/Keukenhof Gardens, Holland; 67 Clive Nichols/Clare Matthews; 68-69 Clive Nichols/Keukenhof Gardens, Holland; 70 top Clive Nichols/Hampton Court 1996/David Stevens; 70 bottom Clive Nichols; 71 Garden Picture Library/Lynne Brotchie; 72-73 Clive Nichols; 74 Clive Nichols/ Keukenhof Gardens, Holland; 75 Clive Nichols; 76-77 Clive Nichols/Lisette Pleasance; 78-79 Clive Nichols/Designer: Louise Hampden; 80 Clive Nichols/Pettifers, Oxfordshire; 81 Clive Nichols/Hampton Court 2001/Jane Rendell/Sarah Tavender; 82 Clive Nichols/ Sheila Stedman; 83 Clive Nichols/Design: Clare Matthews; 84-85 Clive Nichols; 86 Clive Nichols/Chelsea 1997/Bunny Guinness; 87 Clive Nichols; 88 top Clive Nichols/ Sheila Fishwick; 88 bottom Clive

Nichols/Design by Bright Green; 89 Clive Nichols; 90 Clive Nichols/Hampton Court 1998/Natural & Oriental Water Gardens; 91 Clive Nichols/ Chelsea 1999/Carol Klein/Channel 4; 92 Clive Nichols/Wynniatt-Husey Clarke; 93 Clive Nichols/Design: Clare Matthews; 94-95 Clive Nichols/Sheila Fishwick; 96-97 Clive Nichols/Pam Schwert/S Kreutzberger; 98 Clive Nichols/Pettifers, Oxfordshire; 99 Clive Nichols/Bill Smith & Dennis Schrader; 100 Clive Nichols/Designer: John Massey; 101 Clive Nichols/Welbeck; 102 Clive Nichols/Chelsea 1995/Designer: Mark Walker; 103 top Clive Nichols/Stephen Woodhams; 103 bottom Clive Nichols/Chelsea 1998/Emma Lush; 104 Clive Nichols/Hampton Court 2005/Liz Dixon-Spain; 105 top Clive Nichols/ Claire Knight/Linda Pollard; 105 bottom Clive Nichols/Susan Slater; 106-107 Clive Nichols/Clare Matthews; 108 Clive Nichols/Pettifers, Oxfordshire; 109t Clive Nichols/ Amir Schlesinger/My Landscapes; 109b Clive Nichols/Chelsea 1999/Sir Terence Conran; 110-113 Clive Nichols/Clare Matthews; 114-115 Clive Nichols/Steve Grainger; 116 Clive Nichols/Lakemount, Cork, Eire; 117 Clive Nichols/The Nichols Garden, Reading; 118 top Clive Nichols/Hampton Court 1997/HMP Leyhill; 118 bottom Clive Nichols; 119 Clive Nichols/The Nichols Garden, Reading; 120 top Clive Nichols/Claire Mee; 120 bottom Clive Nichols/Colin & Ruth Lorking, Suffolk; 121 Clive Nichols/Welbeck; 122-123 Clive Nichols/The Nichols Garden, Reading; 124-125 Clive Nichols; 126-127 Clive Nichols/Nigel Duff/Greg Riddle; 128 Clive Nichols/The Nichols Garden, Reading; 129 Clive Nichols/Little Coopers, Hampshire; 130 Clive Nichols; 131 Clive Nichols/ Designer: John Massey; 132 left Clive Nichols/Design: Clare Matthews; 132 right Clive Nichols; 133 Clive Nichols/Designer: Jill Billington; 134 Clive Nichols; 135 Clive Nichols/Oxford Botanic Garden; 136 left Clive Nichols/Designer: David Hicks; 136 right Clive Nichols/Jane Nichols; 137 Clive Nichols; 138-139 Clive Nichols/C Cordy; 140-141 Clive Nichols/Keukenhof Gardens, Holland; 142-143 Clive Nichols/Lisette Pleasance